DARK TIMES

Other works by Jonathan Sklar

Landscapes of the Dark: History, Trauma, Psychoanalysis (Karnac, 2011)
Balint Matters: Psychosomatics and the Art of Assessment (Karnac, 2017)

DARK TIMES
Psychoanalytic Perspectives on Politics, History and Mourning

Jonathan Sklar

PHOENIX
PUBLISHING HOUSE
firing the mind

First published in 2019 by
Phoenix Publishing House Ltd
62 Bucknell Road
Bicester
Oxfordshire OX26 2DS

British Library Cataloguing in Publication Data

A C.I.P. for this book is available from the British Library

ISBN-13: 978-1-912691-00-5

Typeset by Medlar Publishing Solutions Pvt Ltd, India

Printed in the United Kingdom

www.phoenixpublishinghouse.co.uk
www.firingthemind.com

Front cover images:
1945: Old Town Warsaw waf-2012-1501-31(1945); https://commons.wikimedia.org/wiki/File:Old_Town_Warsaw_waf-2012-1501-31(1945).jpg
2009: Poland_4076 – Old Town Square by Dennis Jarvis; https://www.flickr.com/photos/archer10/4198069910

For my father

Contents

Preface   ix
About the author   xi
Acknowledgements   xiii
Introduction   xv

Europe in dark times: some dynamics in alterity and prejudice   1

Thinking on the border: memory and trauma in society   25

Cruelty in the early environment and its relationship with racism   53

Epilogue   75
References   79
Index   85

Preface

On Sunday 4 October 1936, the British Union of Fascists (BUF), led by Sir Oswald Mosley, planned a mass rally in the East End of London, a poor area where the majority of Eastern European shtetl Jews had settled since arriving between 1881 and 1914, many having fled anti-Semitic pogroms in Russia, Poland, and other Eastern European countries. These Jews had followed previous waves of immigrants, the Huguenots and the Irish, settling in the same area that today contains a substantial Bengali community. Mosley was backed by a large proportion of the Conservative Party and, responding to appeals to stop the march, Stanley Baldwin, the Prime Minister, said that banning it would be a negation of democracy (Auestad, 2015, pp. 139–140). The 6,000 police officers, including the entire horseback division, escorted the Blackshirts (as the supporters of the BUF were known from the uniforms they wore). The local Irish dockers (remembering the support of the Jewish community in the dock strikes of 1912), the trade unions, and the communists joined the Jews in an antifascist alliance, assembling barricades across Cable Street to halt the fascist march.

The Association of Jewish Ex-Servicemen, marching down Whitechapel Road wearing their medals, found that the police were blocking their path, and ordering them to disperse. Upon refusal, the police began to beat them. By this time, more than 300,000 antifascists had gathered at the point that the Blackshirts would have to pass, shouting *"¡No Pasarán!"* ("They shall not pass!")—the International Brigades' slogan directed at Franco and the Nazis in the Spanish Civil War. The police, attempting to clear the barriers, were met with a shower of stones and other missiles. Eventually, the planned march through the East End was cancelled.

This was a people's victory against the state and a government that had allied itself, at that moment, with the fascists. It was a revolutionary moment. In addition, Mosley's provocation directly led to parliament debating the Public Order Act 1936, which was passed into law on 1 January 1937. The Act banned the wearing of political uniforms in public and demanded that public processions obtain police consent. This hindered the Blackshirts, who enjoyed dressing up in their quasi-military uniform.

I have begun this book full of stories with this story as it was told to me as a child. My father, a serviceman on leave at the time, had been at the barricades, and I marvelled in the romance and felt proud of my father for protecting the Jews and being on the right side of history and politics. One importance that this story occupied for me as I grew up, trying to under-stand the world, was as a reasoned argument that my father had set up a pro-tective shield against anti-Semitism for his future family and children—an act that would cover my lifetime, ensuring safety. Over the years, however, and increasingly so in our modern times, this shield has become fractured and we begin to witness fascism returning from its repressed cavities. As my Serbian friend Marija Vezmar recently wrote to me:

> A thought: how history repeats. The situation in our country seems, believe it or not, never worse and psychoanalysis is, again, my strong-hold. On the surface it's not like in Milošević time, but underneath I feel we're still going down. Maybe it's like that in the whole world?!
> (personal communication, April 2018)

It is crucial that we respond actively to this threat of descent. Indeed, each generation must pick up the political thought and action of confronting fascism when the realisation hits, yet again, that this work is needed. With this task in mind, this book is my attempt to add to the barricades of *¡No Pasarán!*

About the author

Dr Jonathan Sklar, MBBS, FRCPsych is a training and supervising psychoanalyst of the British Psychoanalytical Society. Originally trained in psychiatry at Friern and the Royal Free Hospitals, he later trained in adult psychotherapy at the Tavistock Clinic, London. For many years, he was consultant psychotherapist and head of the psychotherapy department at Addenbrooke's and Fulbourn hospitals in Cambridge.

He now works in full-time analytic practice in London. As well as lecturing widely across the world, he has taught psychoanalysis annually in South Africa for over ten years, termly in Chicago for ten years until 2018, as well as regularly across Eastern Europe. From 2007 to 2011, he was vice president of the European Psychoanalytic Federation, with special responsibility for seminars for recently qualified analysts as well as new analytic groups in East Europe. He has been a board member of the International Psychoanalytical Association since 2015, with his term due to end in July 2019.

Acknowledgements

At the end of my first book, *Landscapes of the Dark: History, Trauma, Psychoanalysis* (2011), I wrote an epilogue that remained in my mind long after the book's publication. Three years later, in 2014, I began to expand on this short piece and the subjects it touches upon. The outcome is this book. It also has the word "dark" in its title, but it has a different focus from that of my earlier book; its subject is psychoanalysis applied to politics and society today. I am grateful to Karnac for permission to reuse and develop further the epilogue from my earlier book.

Much of this book has emerged out of a series of lectures I have given since 2015 in psychoanalytic societies, university departments, and small conferences, the discussions at which enabled further writing.

I want to thank all the participants in Dr Lene Auestad's 2017 conference in Paris, titled *Anxious Encounters and Forces of Fear*; the participants of David Morgan's 2015–2018 *Political Mind* seminars at the Institute of Psychoanalysis in London; Jasminka Šuljagić, Tijana Miladinović, and the Psychoanalytical Society of Serbia; Valentina Lessenska and the Bulgarian Society; and Moisés Lemlij and the participants of the 2018 *La Escena Contemporánea* conference in Lima. I would also like to thank Antal Bokay for hosting me and my paper at Pécs University in Hungary in 2012, and similarly Samir Gandesha at Simon Fraser University, Vancouver, for hosting me in 2015; Dr Ken Robinson of the North of England Association for

Psychoanalytic Psychotherapy for hosting me in 2017 and 2018; and Carla Mantilla for hosting me at the Catholic University of Peru, in Lima in 2018. I am also grateful to Dr Jorge Canestri for encouraging me to present two lectures at the European Psychoanalytical Federation conferences in The Hague and Warsaw, in 2017 and 2018. The three main chapters were also originally lectures given annually at the Institute of Psychoanalysis Summer School Birkbeck, University of London 2016–2018.

I also want to thank the four groups of colleagues that I have been working with termly in Chicago since 2009 for their input into these essays and, in particular, for sharing their thoughts about psychoanalysis in the US.

I am delighted to have been invited by Kate Pearce to publish under Phoenix Publishing House.

Lastly, and most importantly, I want to thank my editor Patrick Davies for his advice, care, and patience with my texts.

The chapter "Thinking on the Border: Memory and the Trauma in Society" is a much-extended essay originally published as the epilogue in my earlier book *Landscapes of the Dark: History, Trauma, Psychoanalysis* (London: Karnac, 2011).

Excerpt from Grossman, D. (2012). D. Grossman interview with D. Aaronovitch. In: *Hay Festival Conversations: Thirty Conversations for Thirty Years*. Hay: Hay Festival Press, 2017. Reprinted with kind permission of David Grossman and Hay Festival Press.

Excerpt from *Selected Poems* by Anna Akhmatova, translated by D.M. Thomas published by Martin Secker & Warburg Limited. Reproduced by permission of The Random House Group Ltd. © 1979.

Introduction

> I perceived ever more clearly that the events of human history, the interactions between human nature, cultural development and the precipitates of primaeval experiences (the most prominent of which is religion) are no more than a reflection of the dynamic conflicts between the ego, the id and the super-ego, which psychoanalysis studies in the individual—are the very same processes repeated upon a wider stage.
>
> —Sigmund Freud, "An Autobiographical Study" (1925d, p. 72)

Psychoanalysts have largely avoided political and social commentary, usually citing the potential for it to be an intrusion into the privacy and confidentiality of the work of the consulting room. Their analytic skills have been perceived to be properly reserved for clinical use, and their application to society seen as rashness. There are, of course, notable exceptions: the writings of Otto Fenichel, Wilhelm Reich, Erich Fromm, Alexander and Margarete Mitscherlich, Marie Langer, and R. D. Laing immediately spring to mind. Freud also turned his analytic considerations towards society, of course, as the epigraph makes clear. However, despite living through the First World War and its aftermath, he did not feel able to speak up in an open way in the late 1920s and 1930s against the totalitarian regime. It is likely that he feared the identification of psychoanalysis as a Jewish science and, as with the burning of his texts in 1933, that fate would envelop the discipline.

Today, with the rise of nationalism, the return of totalitarian parties in Europe to electoral success, and the rise of the alt-right and white supremacists in the US, I believe there is an urgency for psychoanalysts to speak out. The analyst's understanding of the mental mechanisms found in the consulting room—in particular, those of cruelty, sadomasochism, and perversion, which are often rooted in a harmful early environment—can also be applied to the atmospheres that can seem to erupt uncontrollably into society, infecting it and causing profound splits and ruptures, with an "us" vs "them" mentality. Like a mystic writing pad on which marks are preserved from previous writings, to which Freud likened the memory traces of an individual's unconscious (Freud, 1925a), society too retains the capacity for unconscious remembrances to return from the past. Such unconscious shards can erupt seemingly out of nowhere, as disconnects in the minds of both individuals as well as groups of citizens, influencing behaviour and politics. Many commentators have drawn analogies between the political, economic, and social developments of the present and those of 1930s Europe, including the rise of totalitarianism and fascism.

An example of this is Joe Kaeser, chief executive of Siemens, who received death threats in May 2018 after denouncing a speech by Alice Weidel, parliamentary head of the right-wing Alternative for Germany party, in which she labelled refugees as "girls in headscarves … good for nothing". His response: "This isn't about headscarves. It's about discrimination, racism and nationalism." This attitude evoked parallels with the "League of German Girls", the female equivalent of the Hitler Youth in the 1930s and 1940s. He had spoken up now because nobody had spoken up then. Between 1940 and 1945, Siemens used over 80,000 forced labourers, of which at least 5,000 were concentration camp victims (Kaeser, 2018).

Although comparisons to the 1930s and the Second World War are up for debate, the concerns of many people have been heightened by dark memories of that time assailing and preoccupying the mind.

It is interesting to consider the degree to which social oppression or violence can be repressed, states of control sometimes being adopted and sometimes discarded as society lurches towards or away from freedom. The recent departure of Robert Mugabe after 37 years of dominating Zimbabwe led to the great happiness of thousands of people who had been waiting, both in the country and abroad, for years to receive news of regime change. This eruption was similar to that of the citizens of East and West Germany when the Berlin Wall was breached. For years the people had needed to mentally and physically manage this wall, and so the opening of it allowed the hope of freedom—which had previously been held in privacy, dangerous to openly articulate—to become real.

Walls, as boundaries, are interesting metaphors. We all need boundaries, as any parent will attest, and, indeed, as we are all aware from our own childhood experiences. Some of us are lucky enough to have grown up in a family atmosphere with an enlightened understanding: an appreciation of the value of a lightness and meaningfulness with regard to rules and a delight in the development of children. Others, however, grow up in the shadows of cruel and nonsensical restrictions; of attacks and punishments directed both towards thinking and the body, such as beatings or sexual attacks; or of just not being wanted. Political regimes can have similarly divergent atmospheres with regard to the freedoms or restrictions given to certain of its citizens. Is there a freedom for all or is there a split running through society between the haves and the have-nots, the insiders and the outsiders, the rulers and the *Untermenschen*? As in the family, the splits and boundaries in a society can be either benign or pathological, increasing either the freedoms of citizens—or certain groups of citizens—or the controls imposed upon them.

For example, the law in the US has for decades enshrined the value and importance of women's rights over their own bodies, abortion being legalised by the 1973 *Roe* v. *Wade* decision. But there has recently been a sharp shift towards a patriarchal society dismantling those freedoms, aiming to control women's bodies and minds. How strange that this convergence followed the uncovering of Trump's nasty boasts that "I just start kissing them. … I don't even wait. … When you're a star, they let you do it. You can do anything. Grab 'em by the pussy" (Donald Trump *Access Hollywood* tape, 2016), along with the many accusations of sexual harassment or assault levelled at him during the election. In spite of Trump's blanket denial, attempting to shut down debate around his misogynistic leadership, a new atmosphere is prevailing in which women are speaking out and being heard, and this is having a profound impact. A balance of unconscious forces has existed in which complex layers of denial and obfuscation have smothered what was said, done, and reported. It is exhilarating to sense the sudden collapse of these forces and the consequent leap towards greater freedom, away from a sadomasochistic fixity. Perhaps it is the accretion of small victories towards the main imperative of fighting oppression that allows us small aliquots of hope. When enough has been done, we break out of the darkness and into a clearing.

What might Freud have made of these modern-day political and social corruptions? Of the sense of normality settling around the issue of "fake news", for instance, casting a shadow over the governance of many Western and Eastern European nations, as well as that of the "United States" (an obvious misnomer when we consider the disunity between many of those states, particularly around the issue of immigration)?

In the context of these worrying developments, it is perhaps helpful to consider a method of communication and affirmation that will always be available to us: that of irony. As René Major and Chantal Talagrand describe in *Freud: The Unconscious and World Affairs*, Freud made frequent use of irony in his writing, which is comparable to his use of psychoanalysis, both being characterised as a "[giving up of] illusions and thereby [an affirmation of] the triumph of the spirit over life's adversities" (Major & Talagrand, 2018, p. 2).

In *Jokes and Their Relation to the Unconscious*, Freud wrote of this linguistic technique that:

> Its essence lies in saying the opposite of what one intends to convey to the other person, but in sparing him contradiction by making him understand—by one's tone of voice, by some accompanying gesture, or (where writing is concerned) by some stylistic indications—that one means the opposite of what one says. Irony can only be employed when the other person is prepared to hear the opposite, so that he cannot fail to feel an inclination to contradict. As a result of this condition, irony is exposed particularly easily to the danger of being misunderstood. It brings the person who uses it the advantage of enabling him readily to evade the difficulties of direct expression, for instance in invectives. It produces comic pleasure in the hearer, probably because it stirs him into a contradictory expenditure of energy which is at once recognized as being unnecessary.
>
> (Freud, 1905a, p. 174)

In describing irony in this passage, Freud is describing language's capacity to express many meanings that differ between the surface and the unconsciousness of a word or expression. Crucially to our current topic, we can see that this capacity also makes it possible to express oneself under an authoritarian power when it is dangerous to say other than what is expected.

Such pluralities of meaning offend totalitarianism's drive to control. As Major and Talagrand describe, totalitarian language, rather than modifying the vernacular, "invents new speech that establishes a new rule intended to break with tradition" (Major & Talagrand, 2018, p. 2). This is an attempt to limit the multiplicity of meaning in language, and so to control communication and thought.[1] An example of such invented language is the infamous "*Arbeit macht frei*" ("work sets you free"), set into the metal gates at the entrance to Auschwitz and other concentration camps—an attempt to disarm the processions of Jews entering the death camps.[2]

In contrast to this narrowing, irony plays between multiple existing meanings. By doing so, it provides a way of dealing with an intolerable position, allowing one to provisionally accept the force of the regime whilst simultaneously maintaining a resolve to oppose that force and stay faithful to the truth. In this way, irony serves the double purpose of enabling both discreetness and an affirmation of self. It is thus a form of survival in the face of the invitation to agree to oppression, to capitulate to that which is an attack on one's own humanity, dignity, and relationship with reality. Language's inalienable multiplicity will always hold the potential to disrupt the desires and demands of authoritarian regimes to regulate and police meaning. A recent example of the political use of irony is provided by a Shanghai business that makes drinks with darkly comic names and slogans that mock the oppressive regime. "A cup of negative energy a day", for example, plays on President Xi Jinping's slogan "positive energy", with which he appeals to young people to contribute to their country's development (Yang, 2018).

Freud's view, consistent with his use of irony, was that we must face reality rather than live in an illusory world. He did not ignore the waves of savagery gradually engulfing Europe. A sequence listed by Major and Talagrand includes the following events:

> On 22 March 1933, the first concentration camp opened in Dachau, … intended for political opponents of the Nazi regime. On 1 April 1933, the boycott of Jewish businesses and shops came into effect; on 7 April 1933, Jews were forbidden to teach in universities and hold public service jobs. On 26 April 1933, the Gestapo … was established by Hermann Göring. On 2 May 1933, German trade unions were dissolved. On 10 May 1933, a book-burning took place. … The Nazi party become the only party in power … [and] Hitler was elected President, while remaining Chancellor of Germany. On 15 September 1935, the Nuremberg Race Laws were passed, "for the protection of German blood". On 3 March 1936, Jewish doctors were forbidden to practise. … On 13 March 1938, Austria was annexed to the Reich

(*Anschluss*). … On 30 January 1939, Hitler announced "the annihila-
tion of the Jewish race in Europe".

(Major & Talagrand, 2018, pp. 2–3)

It was impossible for Freud to ignore these developments. From 1929 to
1939, he kept a diary of long, loose pages of brief one-line notes describing
what happened each day and covering the family, the world of psychoanalysis, and the politics of Germany and Austria (Molnar, 1992). He wrote to
his close friend, the Dutch analyst Jeanne Lampl-de Groot: "We are all curi-
ous what will come of the program of Reichs Chancellor Hitler, whose only
political theme is pogroms" (ibid., p. 141). Freud is under no illusions here,
playing derisively between "program" and "pogrom". And how brave an
activity that during the decay of institutional systems in Germany between
1933 and 1938, Freud was crafting his ideas on anti-Semitism in *Moses and
Monotheism* (1939a), albeit with anxiety about the impact of its publication
(to be allayed by his departure for freedom to London, following the ran-
som paid to the Third Reich by another close friend and analyst, Princess
Marie Bonaparte). The exile of the unconscious Oedipus is echoed by that
of Freud, although Freud, by contrast, was an exile with a conscious knowledge of himself and his times.

The above sequence outlining the destruction of the rules of state is a
sharp reminder of what can happen as a result of the governance of a particular leader bent on ruling through the imposition of internal states of
prejudice on the nation. This form of governance is increasingly becoming
the norm once again, seen in abusive takeovers of power and reductions in
representative justice in Poland, Hungary, the UK's right-wing Brexiteers,
and America. This book is an attempt to face this reality, and it will meander
with this aim around many diverse themes. Language, with its many obvious or more private meanings, will be a central theme, as will stories—from
fairy tales beloved and feared from childhood to the tellings of impossible
histories that we are led to bear witness to, hearing their many layers of
deeds committed and suffered.

The first chapter focuses on the importance of mourning, listening to
difference, and authentic knowledge in order to preserve freedom and counter systems of control, deceit, and abuse. It also considers attacks on alterity and the dynamics of splitting in society. The second chapter examines
both storytelling and the elision of thought and history in today's world. It
takes a closer look at the dynamics of mourning and considers psychic and

historical gaps, splits, and tears in society, including in the context of anxieties around immigration. This chapter, particularly in its consideration of the brutalities inflicted by ISIS on the Yazidi, is the most visceral of the book. By this, I mean that it was written and will be read in a psychosomatic sense, as some of its descriptions need to be felt in the body (reflecting Freud's early idea that the original ego was the body ego). These feelings can overwhelm the capacity of the conscious mind to take them in, yet to my mind there is still a need to notice them. The third chapter is a meditation on the relationship between cruelty in the early environment and hatred of the other within society, looking particularly at racism in the US.

Although small, this book goes against the grain of the current trend for brief soundbites that allow us to pass swiftly over painful information. It will go into the details of some extremely dark occurrences, not to glorify cruelties, but in order to understand them, as well as to give thought to the individuals who have suffered them. In turn, this will provide the reader with greater access to things residing in the unconscious. It will, hopefully, also allow the reader to become more in touch with the humanity in human beings—with qualities that totalitarian mentalities prefer buried, so they do not hinder our loyalty to the regime.

Listening to stories such as those collected within this book enables us to become more aware, not only of what is going on *over there*, but also what is happening *here*. In our increasingly joined-up world, *here* is always implicated and affected too. My hope is that the reader will be brave enough to listen, and to face disrupting the illusions of our political times. Ridding ourselves of these illusions is crucial if we are to find the freedom to think, develop, challenge, and create hope—for future generations, as well as for ourselves.

Endnotes

1. This drive is examined amply by the philologist Victor Klemperer in *The Language of the Third Reich* (1957), following Nazism's destructuring of language and reduction of German thought and culture into new, narrow meanings.
2. One could perhaps call this an irony, of course, but this is a perverse and vicious text.

Europe in dark times
some dynamics in alterity and prejudice

In the fearful years of the Yezhov terror I spent seventeen months in prison queues in Leningrad. One day somebody "identified" me. Beside me, in the queue, there was a woman with blue lips. She had, of course, never heard of me; but she suddenly came out of that trance so common to us all and whispered in my ear (everybody spoke in whispers there): "Can you describe this?" And I said: "Yes, I can." And then something like the shadow of a smile crossed what had once been her face.
—Anna Akhmatova, 1 April 1957, Leningrad, *Requiem* (p. 67)

Today's Europe, with its recent explosion of immigration, bringing the mass death of children and adults on our shores, invites a return of the repressed and the blaming of the *Untermenschen* for our difficulties. Our remembrances of history as recent as the 1930s, and the link between austerity and blame, are leading to a wholesale diminution of our humanity. Facts have become no longer recognised—most apparent in the recent Brexit referendum and the presidential election in the US—as have the views of those with expertise. Right-wing political movements regularly brush aside criticism, or any inconvenient knowledge, as being of no value. Such things occurred in the 1930s and made possible the rhetoric that stoked the rise of fascism.

In this first chapter, against the backdrop of these events, I want to examine states of freedom in mental life. This will involve examining states of

1

fundamentalism in twentieth-century society, along with some of their specific impacts, in particular on psychoanalysis and psychoanalytic societies. I will then turn my attention towards alterity—the problem of the other—and how we might understand the massive attacks on migrants entering and living in our worlds, as well as the impact of these attacks on citizens.

The examination of impediments to social freedom has parallels with the process of developing states of mental freedom, in both analysis and the analyst, that exist in the unconscious mind—that is, freedom from the stickiness of our personal histories, freedom within the society that trained us, and freedom from the often unspoken depths of our European culture. Such complex matters include the need for the analysand to find new ways of expression, both in relation to him or herself and in relation to the other, and so to no longer follow the old tramways of habits laid down by personal histories, which can become caught up in and repeated by the transference dynamic.

In another order, these matters include the question of how best the analyst can develop his or her personal practice of psychoanalysis in a place that may be hostile to such a project. This latter situation unfortunately seems to be becoming more prevalent, certainly in the National Health Service in the UK. Here, I have observed psychodynamic therapy to be virtually wiped out. In its place, low-cost "quick fixes" to get people back to work, regardless of the longer-term efficacy or suitability. The government publically pledges its support for mental health issues. Yet its proposed reforms for improving mental health care have been damned by two select committees as lacking ambition and failing to take into account the needs of the most vulnerable groups (Busby, 9 May 2018). The government provides money for adolescent psychiatric services that is not ring fenced and is often redirected to general resources. Waiting times for a young person to be seen for diagnosis as well as treatment is very lengthy. It is in this environment that the mental health professional must try to find a way to work effectively.

Another central aspect that this discussion must examine is the theory and practice of psychoanalysis itself, along with its training. They both have their own unconscious tramways.

Yet the very theme of freedom alongside my associated word "tramways" first leads my thoughts to the railway lines crossing Europe that were used for transportation to the death camps in the Second World War. European culture, like the human subject, has never been free of aggression, stretching from medieval times through the Enlightenment and culminating in the world wars fought on our soil in the twentieth century, and this has played its part in the evolution of psychoanalysis throughout Europe. Freud, having lived through the First World War, was faced with trying to understand the mass slaughter of nationals—despite, or due to, their cultural heritage—and decades later, in 1938, he had to flee Nazi Vienna. His sisters did not escape and died in concentration camps. What would it have meant for the future development of psychoanalysis if the Nazis had killed the Father?

Taking these facts into account, how can we think about trauma in the individual without thinking of it in generational terms, as well as in terms of the cultural heritage forming the backdrop to the development of psychoanalysis from within the Austro-Hungarian Empire? One of my key interests is the interface between personal and historical trauma, and in particular the relation of such traumatic substrates with unconscious processes. What we can grasp of the innermost life of the patient and of the world he or she lives in, and by which he or she is so profoundly affected, is also part of a broader picture in which ontogeny—the development of an individual's history—is entwined with specific cultures.

Psychologies of prejudice

In terms of European culture, the continent has continuously struggled with the idea of the stranger coming from the East, ready to pollute and destroy the Western order. Each country, in its particular form, has at some point declared itself as a bulwark against the horde: France with its back to the Atlantic against the Germanic tribes, the Goths and the Visigoths, and the Mongol horde beyond; Spain and Portugal similarly fearing the caliphate expansion, as the successful Muslim invasion created Al-Andalus; and Germany against the atheist Communists in Russia, as well as the impoverished villages of Poland and the Eastern states dotted with shtetl Jews. This history can also be seen through the opposite lens: the Roman legions spreading the Empire far to the east, along with the many crusades invading the Middle East. Throughout such conflicts ran the conviction that it is cities that are civilised (*civitas*), while the wanderer is impure, dangerous, and stupid. Strong boundaries are similarly an essential component of the nation state, advancing the same psychology of us vs them, and of demonising the other; this system having at its core a psychology of prejudice.

In an attempt to counter this tendency, the European Union, despite considerable internal stresses, maintains justice for all of its citizens as its core value, enforcing it in the European Court of Justice and bound by the European Convention of Human Rights. These ethical and democratic structures transcend the boundaries of the nation states of the Union and are a profound answer to each of their vicissitudes and particularities. It is important to remember that they were set up, in particular, as a bulwark against another war in Europe. Yet the still underlying, latent fears and desires that form prejudice towards the other await their return from repression by such structures.

Unconscious prejudicial phantasies can relate similarly to analytic societies in terms of wishes to accentuate particular forms of analytic theory and training. The wish for a widespread development of training that focuses on one method or perspective can neglect the particular analytic sense of the individual treatment. It can thus appear more important for the analyst to hold on to theory, fearing becoming lost or fearing a state of free fall in the face of not understanding something in or from the analysand. Analysis often comprises finding and sustaining hard-won pieces of knowledge, wrestled from the unconscious, that act as a psychic pointillism or patchwork, slowly connecting in some way as the creative act of the analysis.

Widening the analytic lens so that we can examine such unconscious patchwork with regard to the discipline of psychoanalysis in the European region, we can note present-day concerns, in the current climate of quick fixes and business solutions, about its very survival as a form of treatment. Yet by looking back in history, we can see that psychoanalysis has often had the unstable status of being an unwelcomed other. Indeed, Freud's fear was that it could be attacked and demoted if the scientific community, as well as the Nazi state, perceived it to be a Jewish theory. He never let go of the worry that the eruption of the workings of unconscious life (through psychoanalysis) had occurred within a dialectic that entailed their return to a state of repression—especially if it came to be perceived as having a negative influence in society. This was, in part, the focus of Freud's concern with apostasy among some of his followers.

Knowledge of the unconscious does not have to lead to its subsequent destruction in society, however, despite programmes now abounding that demand quick changes in symptomatology following external modelling, such as the positivistic thinking of cognitive behavioural therapy (CBT), or the impact of an early and fragile positive transference. One positive result of these superficial tendencies is that it is difficult now to really destroy psychoanalysis. Its status is too present, delineated especially by the fact that it is worth attacking because it still exists, albeit as an underground subject.

Some scars in European psychoanalytic societies

It is important to acknowledge that European analytical societies, including those formed around the birth of psychoanalysis, have often emerged, either sooner or later, from profound historical traumas—events that, for many of us, remain part of our own lifetimes. These histories constitute our psychosocial cultural tramways and they can exist in states of repression, or can sometimes, through a reckoning with history, allow the emergence of a new order.

The many years that populations were under rigid control systems (such as in Nazi Germany, Communist East Europe, and racist South Africa) have had their impact—lasting effects of things that could not be spoken or expressed, either in the family or on the streets, without the enormous fear of the network of local spies and party members, and so of punishment. These past aggressive political controls were essentially ways of bullying the other on a grand scale, and they have deeply penetrated family life, schools, and workplaces, in so doing provoking the development of unconscious ways of coping.

Over the last century, the many countries that have had repressive governments have now seen generations of children grow up in paranoid atmospheres, especially so at home, whereby the practice of keeping silent was maintained so that children would not be able to say anything dangerous about their parents' views when outside. Such protective social mechanisms can become what appear as an "ordinary sensible" paranoia.

In the analysis of candidates who grew up under totalitarian regimes—such as Nazi, Stalinist, or South African—the germ of the paranoia needs to have especial notice taken of it. It is ubiquitous, often silent, and with an appearance of being ordinary. To escape such mental attack, such analysands need to question not only their own history, but also that of the analyst—where he or she has come from, and what their imagined trauma has been. This is to ensure that a conformative transference is not just a passive acceptance of a training control system that might be unconsciously perceived as similar to the old nationalist repressive regime. How would one know that the old regime has been overthrown, unless there is authentic freedom in the analytic consulting room, and not just an assumption that all is well? Paranoia invariably lives out its existence underground, beneath a pseudo-normative false self.

Such important analytic work is conducted not through question and answer, but rather through what became known in South Africa as "truth and reconciliation": a process of searching out and giving description to the traumatic landscapes where so many bodies had been secretly buried, away from the families' knowledge. Totalitarian regimes, and their deep controls embedded in social, political, and family life, still play their parts in the unconscious dynamics of twenty-first-century cultural life, as do the wars within some parts of Europe, including those which have only recently ended, for the time being (although one is still being fought between Ukraine and Russia).

It is the scars from such histories that also run through many European analytic societies. For example, the Berlin Psychoanalytic Institute and the impact of the steady departure of Jewish analysts under Nazism. As Eran J. Rolnik writes, "it was clear from the beginning of Nazi rule that Jewish analysts would not be permitted to remain in the country" (Rolnik, 2012, p. 82). The departure of Max Eitingon, the strong and diligent president of the society, loyal to Freud, was particularly painful, prompting Freud to write on 23 August 1933, to Ernest Jones, that "Berlin is Lost" (ibid., p. 83). Felix Boehm, Eitingon's successor, struggled to maintain the survival of the Institute as an environment in which Jewish and non-Jewish analysts could work together, holding it up as an anomaly in Nazi Germany, yet, at the same time, working hard to ensure that psychoanalysis was kept free from any direct link to Judaism (ibid., pp. 89–90). This inevitably caused tensions in the international psychoanalytic community, one particularly incendiary incident being the Institute's response following the arrest of the young Jewish analyst Edith Jacobson, whose ties with Communist resistance had been discovered by the Gestapo (ibid., pp. 88–89).

In reaction to the ensuing international criticism, Boehm explained his decision not to come out in defence of Jacobson in terms of his attempts to dissociate the Institute from both Judaism and political resistance (ibid., pp. 88–89). His attempts at maintaining the Institute as an island in which Jews could still practise did not survive much longer, however, and by 1936 it was annexed to the German Institute for Psychological Research and Psychotherapy (ibid., p. 90). This was the so-called "Göring Institute", its director Matthias Göring being the nephew of Field Marshall Hermann Göring.

Here, Boehm, Göring, and Carl Müller-Braunschweig, along with a further fourteen non-Jewish members of the Institute, went on to develop a significantly altered form of "psychoanalysis" that was compatible with Nazi ideology (the Institute's one surviving copy of Freud's works was locked away in a cupboard known as "the poison cabinet") (ibid., p. 90–91).

As Rolnik concludes,

> German psychoanalysts did not display unusual resilience in standing up to the regime's demands. The Berlin Psychoanalytic Institute fell victim to the official Nazi policy of anti-Jewish discrimination at a relatively early stage. (ibid., p. 91)

In truth, the original psychoanalytic societies of Berlin and Vienna were destroyed and replaced, as if seamlessly and unnoticed, by monsters that covered over the gap.

It is worth noting here that Freud was well aware of the profound impact that Nazism and its anti-Semitic policies were having on every aspect of life, and that he dedicated a major part of his late writings, in *Moses and Monotheism* (which was written in 1934, revised in 1936, and then published in 1938), to analysing the foundations of anti-Semitism. In the first preface of this book, he describes Nazism as "a relapse into almost prehistoric barbarism" (Freud, 1939a, p. 54). It is likely that Freud's powerful description here refers to the Nazi use of power to severely limit and curtail the lives and careers of Jews. Seeing that the surface propaganda was an illusion, he faced the truth of the attacks that were occurring. As Freud wrote in a letter to Romain Rolland: "A great part of my life's work has been spent (trying to) destroy illusions of my own and those of mankind" (Freud, 4 March 1923, p. 346).

The impact of the discrimination, anti-Semitism, and intimidation of Nazism has lasted long after its defeat. In March 2018, the European Psychoanalytical Federation (EPF) held its annual conference in Warsaw. At the same time, the right-wing government was bringing in legislation to criminalise any assertion of Polish involvement in the Holocaust or other war crimes occurring under the German occupation of the Second World War. This created a profound sense of anxiety in advance of the conference. Many analysts even preferred not to attend. Others felt the opposite, however: that in the face of such anti-Semitism, they must attend, specifically in order to stand up to the corruption of Polish ideology. With a similar mindset, I realised that it would be valuable to one day hold a conference titled "Psychoanalysis and Anti-Semitism". This would defiantly counter the historical anti-Semitic attacks on the "Jewish science" of psychoanalysis, which have not diminished to this day (even Freud fell into this perception, holding Jung in such high esteem partly because he was not Jewish).

At the conference, I read the next chapter of this book as a lecture, including the material about anti-Semitism in Poland. There was clearly a great deal of anxiety in the conference about what might or might not be spoken about, and, while I did not think I would be arrested for my remarks in the middle of a conference in Warsaw, this phantasy was tangibly present.

Near the end of the conference, I attended a large group discussion about the meaning and feeling of meeting together in Warsaw. Around 100 analysts sat in a large spiral for 90 minutes and spoke their thoughts. Many expressed their sense of the dead rising from the ground, evoked by the areas still empty and covered with rubble that are parts of the destroyed ghetto; by the horrors written on the tombstones of the old Jewish cemetery; and by the two parts of the ghetto wall that remain standing. The chill was palpable.

Towards the end of the discussion, I spoke of my great concern about the rise of totalitarian states of mind in governments in Europe, the US, and elsewhere, and said that I found the return of Nazism very frightening. I then asserted that it is essential that analysts draw attention to how the mental states of cruelty, sadomasochism, perversion, and identification with the aggressor—which we know and work with in our consulting rooms—can also pervade society. To my horror, not a single colleague responded to my remarks and I was left isolated and alone with my concerns. I later realised that the room was filled with fear—not of the past but for the future—and that the roomful of analysts were unable to process their group affect. The scars are still with us today.

The fall of the Berlin Wall and contrapuntal listening

With the fall of the Berlin Wall and the reopening of Europe from East to West and West to East, the continent has an increased historical and cultural heterogeneity, as we must now take account of the impact of totalitarian regimes on countries that lived behind the Iron Curtain. As a result, analytic training has become much more complex.

Without doubt, Europe has been the leading arena for the development of new analytic societies. Young people suddenly finding themselves in a position with the freedom to think outside of the old regime's rules were at once attracted to psychoanalysis as a place to begin to think freely and to ascertain the damage that had been done to their self, their family, and their culture. Many new analytic societies thus soon formed in Eastern Europe following the collapse of Communism, making treatment available where it was once proscribed.

In conjunction with this, forms of organisation and meeting in the EPF have become part of something profound with regard to negotiating difference—first, acting as ways of breaking down the sense of a large, monolithic organisation into more manageable and approachable resources, but, critically, second, enabling a realisation that no single analytic training contains the truth of analysis. Learning the many ways of approaching the patient is a great antidote to the narcissisms of both small and large differences, and so these regular meetings outside particular analytic societies are an essential resource for the future development of analysis in a growing and complex region.

What we have been establishing with these approaches is a new form that is not only about learning more about the complexities of psychoanalysis but that also allows us to begin to listen "contrapuntally"—a musical term adapted by Edward Said to describe a way of creatively negotiating and discriminating between what can often be profoundly divergent ways of understanding both theory and practice. This type of listening implies that the barrier to recognition, often a result of ignorance, or of ignoring that which we do not imagine of the other, becomes something to be faced, confronted, and argued against within a facilitating environment. It also implies that profound cultural differences can be noticed and explored.

Such listening attempts to overcome what we do not imagine of the other—that which is consequently unavailable for us to process and integrate into understanding. Prejudice relies on stereotypes of otherness, which appear to demand that we know things of the other that are not true. To form patches of truth requires the breakdown of prejudicial unconscious phantasies that can be deeply held constructs, passed down the generations like unprocessed childhood trauma—doing to and being done to ad infinitum.

We can note similarities here between the way that rigidities and prejudices can be passed on in both analytic societies and wider society, and the way in which systems of mothering can be passed on down the generations. In relation to the baby within the particular dyadic culture that the mother brings, the mother's history of being mothered, as well as *her* mother's history of being mothered, can be rigidly encased as a transgenerational unconscious system. Of course, this can be a benign environment that nourishes development and appropriate separations. Yet even the mother who is unable to be other than an identificate of her own negativistic mother might find, in conjunction with her baby, a new dyadic culture in early formation, allowing the development of what Michael Balint called a "new beginning". This possibility of new beginnings applies equally to the contexts of wider society and analytic societies, in which there is the same requirement for the collapse of a previously internalised regime that is tough, unquestioned, and fixed.

In psychoanalysis, different theories are different forms of perception, each deserving appropriate understanding and respect. Nonetheless, some positions impede the spirit of analytic neutrality and interfere with free association, in doing so blocking access to a wider range of analytic ideas. What might be called an ethics of listening applies: in our listening to the conscious and to the unconscious, to work both with analysands and with colleagues. To acknowledge the many differing concepts of mind and relationships in psychoanalysis is a further application of the ethics of listening.

In the EPF, there are not only many types and theories of analytic training and clinical practice, but also many languages spoken and heard. I see it as a crucible where these ideas might be developed into a new European analytic dialogue that, in its openness, would be truly in the spirit of Freud's legacy. The capacity to speak together ethically is the best way of preventing authoritarianism in our analytic practice, in our analytic societies, and in our future European history.

To take a brief example, we can consider the difficulties of listening to a colleague describing their own clinical work using a theoretical frame that might differ considerably from our own. To listen only within a singular theoretical construction might well—through its ideas, its direction of the treatment, whether it uses or does not use regression, and whether it has or does not have a historical-developmental understanding—profoundly impact on how one hears the other. This is arguably an ethical problem, as it requires a particular type of listening that is similar to the analyst's listening to the analysand, with evenly suspended attention, not knowing where one is or where one is going. If one listens to the other's clinical material only through one's particular theoretical frame, it is possible to miss the clinical meanings—for instance, only privileging material through the here-and-now transference, which might not be the reporting analyst's position.

It might well require relinquishing a particular knowledge of theory that has become part of one's unconscious mindset, in order to be able to meet the other in the discourse.

Of course, it can be so much easier to invoke one's own theoretical stance to attack the work of the other and to avoid having to think in a different way. Analytic societies can get into a habit of suspending thinking and opting for a simpler, political solution—one wrapped up as disdain for a differing analytic theory. In such matters, colleagues can become cruel to fellow members with a differing theoretical leaning, and societies can split. In order to throw another light on this matter, I want to quote from the 1995 Nobel Prize lecture by Seamus Heaney, who writes of the need to find an appropriate balance of contradictory positions:

> The need on the one hand for a truth telling that will be hard and retributive, and on the other hand, the need not to harden the mind to a point where it denies its own yearnings for sweetness and trust.
>
> (Heaney, 1995)

This describes the requirements for a contrapuntal world, of words that need to be spoken and longings that must be recognised, a world that might be thought in terms of Ferenczi's "elasticity" (his expression of the analytic concept of tact), holding the tensions, as they differ from time to time, both in analysis and within society. A certain amount of elasticity is required to listen beyond the preconceptions of one's own theoretical frame to make chains of associations possible beyond an early crystallisation of what one thinks one knows. Humble free association is part of such an elastic position that need not harden the mind.

Totalitarian language and political deceit

Totalitarian language is forged in opposition to such an openness and flexibility of thought; it has a particular meaning that must be adhered to, even if it is evidentially incorrect. This is the antithesis of the Freudian invention, which allows the multiplicity of understandings within speech and writing to be noticed and expressed. Under totalitarian regimes, an unconscious master–slave mentality, such as that which governed the Berlin Institute's conformity to Nazi ideology, seeps into language, as George Orwell clearly noticed. Words can often express their very opposite, and repressive, totalitarian regimes abuse this elasticity to pervert and police their subjects' perception and communication of reality. Such systems, the surveillance within them, and the resulting atmosphere of paranoia, can develop in an environment of cascading political lying.

In this context, it is alarming to witness today's politicians reducing complex discussion to often false sound bites, feeding them to the people, who accept them willingly. Brexiteers argue that payments to the EU, totalling millions each week, could, post-Brexit, be directed solely towards saving the National Health Service—blatantly obscuring the fact that a large proportion of those millions is already spent within the UK, with the EU directing back much of the UK's gross payment to meet other funding needs. And right-wing politicians flaunt their supposed concern for the poor, for the health service, and for universities, while simultaneously cutting financial resources in order to apparently balance the budget, affirming that this destruction of hard-won resources in healthcare and education, and the erosion of the savings of ordinary citizens, is good for us. Meanwhile, David Cameron's Brexit legacy is one that weakens and diminishes the European project at a time when standing together would be the intelligent response to the consistent and murderous attacks taking place in many European countries. This political atmosphere of lies and deceit has led to a sense that we can believe what we like, as long as it is not an expert opinion, and so homespun ideology has become the superior currency.

Trauma, mourning, and monuments

In contrast to these tendencies of control, deceit, and linguistic rigidity, within a master–slave mentality, psychoanalysis offers a path towards truth and reconciliation, and away from paranoid discourses towards alterity. The development of the ability to tolerate the other, without allowing domination, and at the same time as recognising complexity, is the modern heritage of psychoanalysis.

In psychoanalysis lies the potential for freedom. This includes the possibility of attaining a more mature position that recognises the vitality of mourning. Creative separation, together with mourning, is a necessary element in the development of the parent–child relationship. The analyst–patient relationship, through unconscious communication, enables this to take place beyond and despite trauma. Where there has been substantial trauma and deprivation, the analytic situation is one that entails the possibility of new formations, which require a bedrock of trust. This can lead to a sense of reparation that sometimes needs to come from the analyst, as a humane and free other—someone who can not only think and understand outside the tramways, but who can be alive outside of them.

Such new formations can also be possible in a traumatised analytic society—for example, if it is able to struggle to mourn its specific historic confrontations between colleagues, rather than surrendering to years of low murmurings of discontent. Attempts at mourning in larger society include the erection of symbols, often statues for remembrance, in either prominent or less obvious positions, but these can often exist for glorification or political dissemination, or can stand "as if" they represent an invitation to remember, and there can be a similar elision of mourning within an analytic society.

Given the traumas of European history and the often intolerant matrix of beliefs maintained within analytic societies, working between societies and countries is bound to touch upon questions of mourning, and can also provide a space for it to be expressed. If such difficult psychic processes, born of all our different but convergent histories in the twentieth and twenty-first centuries, cannot be reflected in the thought and practice within our analytic societies, then where else? This was the central question that international psychoanalysis had to face when returning to Germany for the first time following the Second World War. It was given particular consideration at the 34th International Psychoanalytical Congress in Hamburg in 1985. What value could psychoanalysis have if the analytic community could not face such profound difficulties?

To give an example in which working across boundaries brought about a consideration of mourning, in June 2010, at one of the EPF annual clinical meetings, I was involved in organising a weekend seminar for recently qualified analysts, to take place in Warsaw. Twenty-eight colleagues from analytic societies all over Europe attended and presented clinical analytic material in small groups to a panel of training supervisors. The location was evocative. On the first evening, many of the group enjoyed being in the beautiful, Old Town square, which was completely rebuilt in the post-war reconstruction. They did not realise that this old centre, seemingly so well-kept and ancient, was in fact a deception. A quarter of the city had contained the Warsaw Ghetto, which was totally razed during the 1943 Jewish uprising. In the following year, most of the central parts of the city were also razed during the Polish resistance partisans' uprising against the

Nazi occupation, before the Red Army advanced into Warsaw. Eighty-five per cent of the city was demolished. Following the war, in the early 1950s, the city was lovingly recreated, Canaletto's famous views of the original city being used as the main reference.

In this process of complete reconstruction in Warsaw, we can read the societal and cultural equivalent of the way in which an individual's trauma can be covered up, suppressed, and then detached from any possibility of understanding, such that it can be viewed only from outside as a façade. Unaware of the history, the visitor delights in the perfectly reconstructed medieval environment. Yet what is this Disneyesque reconstruction, which hardly shows any link to the city's real past? The enjoyment of the repaired centre indicates a necessity to not remember, a need to be beguiled by the surface pleasures in sight.

In the centre of the Old Town, outside the castle, is a small photo of the site in 1945 showing almost nothing of this vast building; only a forlorn gateway with its right-hand corner just a tottering thin pile of bricks. Nothing else is standing. A sea of rubble—a horrid and eloquent metaphor of what had happened here earlier… Time has now moved on. The castle and square are fully reconstructed, ignoring what occurred there in the Second World War. This has a symmetry with the neurotic individual who must repress that which cannot be known, because knowledge is apparently too terrible to be made manifest. Knowing the destruction that has occurred means that what one gazes upon holds within its view that which was wiped out. It exists in the negative shadow of what we see before us, as it is this absence that subsists as the trace of the destructive order. In relation to psychosis, Freud describes that "the delusion is found applied like a patch over the place where originally a rent had appeared in the ego's relation to the external world" (Freud 1924, p. 151). Similarly, this European city has applied "a patch over the place where originally a rent had appeared" to cover the absence. Its citizens, and perhaps its visitors, cannot bear to contemplate the tear in their own past, and in their own population, unless courageous mental work is undertaken.

Such patches of architectural memory can be found all over Europe, the only partly recognised signs of a missing history in many important landscapes. In many Spanish cities and towns, for example, there are streets named "Calle Judia" ("Jewish street"); the only remaining signs that Jews once lived there, before their mass expulsion under the Alhambra Decree of 1492, ordered by Queen Isabella and King Ferdinand. All other traces of that history have been completely wiped out. It has not been easy to build the edifices that enable us to mourn our bloody European heritage and provide an atmosphere to facilitate such mourning (see Young, 1993). Germany has had a long journey on this path, from the Mitscherlichs' important book *The Inability to Mourn* in 1967, which analysed the failure of the German people and German society to acknowledge the crimes committed in the name of National Socialism, to the Berlin of today. Alexander Mitscherlich's earlier book, with Fred Mielke, *Doctors of Infamy: The Story of the Nazi Medical Crimes*, when first published in 1949, so inflamed much of society that large numbers were bought up by the German Medical Society in order to suppress it. This society, of course, has its own horrific history—that is, the Nazi medical experiments in many concentration camps, and in particular those conducted by Dr Mengele on twins.

Among the Berlin monuments that exist to remind citizens of the totalitarian past, there are two that strike me as being of particular interest, although perhaps only one of them is truly significant or effective in this context. The first is at Bebelplatz, the site at which, on 10 May 1933, the Nazis burnt 20,000 books, including works by Freud. Today, there is a line written on a plaque in the square, taken from Heinrich Heine's 1820 play *Almansor*: "*Das war ein Vorspiel nur; dort wo man Bücher verbrennt, verbrennt man am Ende auch Menschen*" ("That was only a prelude; where they burn books, they will also ultimately burn people"). The plaque is accompanied by a monument by Micha Ullman consisting of a small glass window set flat into the cobblestones and looking deep underground into an empty library with rows of bare shelves. Evocative, certainly, yet as one walks away from the site, to any distance, it becomes invisible. The ordinary passer-by is not even aware that it is there, so the event is certainly remembered, but only if one is standing in just the right place. The dictum "out of sight, out of mind" occurs to me. If one is aware, prior to visiting, of the destruction that occurred here, or if one just happens to come across it, then it can have a powerful effect. But it is a monument that is easy to ignore.

The second monument is by Peter Eisenman. Commemorating the Holocaust, it consists of 2,711 concrete slabs near the Brandenburg Gate. This is a public work, not hidden away but daily in the sight of all who pass by it in the very centre of the city. It points the way unequivocally and unavoidably to that which is known and needs to be seen, a constant confrontation with destruction, in this way playing an essential part in the regeneration of national soul and spirit. The prose of Anna Akhmatova in the epigraph at the start of this chapter bears testimony to daring to be able to describe that which is so painful, nearly too painful for us to bear bringing it, in words, into the present. And yet, it can be done.

Dissonant landscapes

We can relate this question of historical trauma, and how it is either registered or refused by the mind, to the analytic process. All crises, historical and personal, are both endings and beginnings. In time, the existence of a crisis allows for the development of thoughts both of the origins of the crisis and of how it might end. There is always something unpredictable about this, as well as potentially unsettling—even radically so. To take a metaphor, the apparently simple commencement of a Beethoven symphony can evoke an unconscious expectation, not just of its development, but also of how the composer will be able to dare end what he has created. We find that great works often end in a dissonant way in relation to our milder, more humdrum expectations, exposing the listener to the shock of another, different resolution. Similarly, free association contains the potential for a radical edge that can move us further and further away from the neat narrative hedgerows of conscious life. In doing so, it allows us to find a dissonant landscape, and not necessarily the one we might have tried to creep towards. With understanding, free association can place us at such cardinal positions; we then have to try to understand where we are. These places are different from those where we want to be or desire to be, and indeed often from where society demands that we be. We may be finding shards of an unthought, unspoken traumatic vista, emerging from the analysand's past like a haunting.

This is the reason why all totalitarian regimes detest the possibility of thinking for oneself: because it allows one to break away from the group narrative and the control system of abuse. Again, we can draw an analogy with the role of the analyst in their enabling of free associations that reveal traumatic material deep under the surface. Some analysands can act in a similar way to a dissident in the ranks, breaking free from the dominant, known rhetoric of family life. Issues of dominance and passivity are a common facet of family life, spread around the various players. The analyst is unconsciously expected to play a double role, on the one hand quietly part of that old regime, while on the other being in a separate mental place—one that enables them to notice and help either create or accept a disturbance from the fixity that has hitherto ruled the family and their individual mental states. This process is never easy. It would be wrong to view the end of an analysis, or the end of this chapter, as offering a simple resolution: "all's well that ends well". Psychoanalysis does not deliver cures. However, its instruments do enable the possibility, if we are brave enough to examine the contents of Pandora's box, of finding hope in knowledge.

"Confusion of Tongues" and the splittings of the mind and society

The mourning of historical trauma, however, like all mourning, requires authentic knowledge of what took place, and that the trauma is openly known about, engaged with, and understood. In an attempt to understand, then, let us turn to one of the things from Pandora's box: the problem we all have with the other, around the concept of alterity. For this I want to go back to the arguments between Freud and Sándor Ferenczi in the early 1930s, coinciding with the rise of Hitler, and domination by totalitarian politics.

Freud feared a rejection of his core ideas of unconscious life, especially of the base that he had established in the unconscious oedipal phantasy. Ferenczi, however, while always a Freudian and accepting the unconscious phantasy structure of the Oedipus complex, was also concerned with those many patients who had experienced an environmental deficiency through an early infantile trauma. He felt that these patients required a new technique to deal with the pre-oedipal loss of basic trust, and other concomitant issues.

In a paper concerned with such early traumas, "Confusion of Tongues between Adults and the Child" (1933), Ferenczi shows in a radical way the structure of abuse between the adult and the child. It describes the biphasic attack on the child, beginning in a guise of playfulness that excites the child, desirous of the attention of the grown up, who grooms the way for a sexual assault that may end in penetration. By this point, the child is at best confused, at worst in pain, and Ferenczi describes how the child can protect him or herself from the impact of the attack—an attack on both trust and the body—by a split in the ego. "That is not really happening to me, just to my body." Or the child can look intensely at the pattern of the wallpaper or the curtains in an attempt to separate themselves from what is happening in the room. The child becomes lost and missing as a deep defence from the pain of the onslaught. However, Ferenczi now brings out the other, arguably worse, trauma: the adult repudiating what has just occurred, often telling the child, "It is only your imagination," or saying, "Look what you made me do—it's your fault," and "Don't tell anyone our secret—if you do, nobody will believe you." This even more vicious, second assault is now on the mind of the child. Reality is attacked and the child is detached from anyone who might help and listen, told that they will not be believed. They are invited to understand that it is really all an incident about nothing. This is an attack on thinking—on reality—and it invariably leaves the victim alone, hurt, and confused, and with severe difficulties regarding basic trust.

All this deals with the subject of paedophilia in a way that, when the paper is read for the first time, feels contemporary, despite having been written in 1933. It helps us to understand the psychology of splitting in the defence of the ego, pursued at the cost of forming an internal state of alienation and a carapace in the child's character, leading to great fear in the child, and then adult, around trusting in the world and in relationships. Anna Freud developed Ferenczi's ideas further, describing an additional mechanism of defence resulting in an identification with the aggressor (see A. Freud, 1936). This is the common history of many paedophiles, often having been abused as children themselves.

We can apply the same dynamic steps to understanding the attacks on alterity with anti-Semitism, Islamophobia, racism, misogyny, and homophobia. For instance, a group of colleagues are meeting together and suddenly one tells an anti-Semitic joke, in the knowledge that one of the group is Jewish. Everyone but the Jew may laugh, and he might feel helpless at being, at that moment, not part of the group, unless he tries to signal with laughter that he is part of it. Perhaps he becomes angry about the cruel and crude stereotyping, and, being an adult, he might well decide to speak up. If he protests, the anti-Semite can quickly riposte that it was only a joke, nothing was meant by it, and the Jew is just oversensitive. Here we can see the second attack, as in paedophilia, where the evidence in front of the victim is dismissed as not being real. The attack continues to proceed with the idea that the Jew is just too thin-skinned. This has a further meaning, that there is no anti-Semitic attack, only that he (a Jew) has a problem with humour. It is a double attack that, as with the child, leaves the victim in a state of alienation from the group.

This unconscious dynamic also plays out in racist and homophobic attacks where the victim is insulted and then informed that they took a wrong and unintended meaning. Such victims are told that any racist or homophobic meaning is the product of their own misunderstanding, and so, far from being a victim, they are in fact the architects of their own difficulty, and, furthermore, are not like "us", who can understand jokes and are adult enough to not misunderstand what is being said.

In 2012, fascist Serbian football supporters, watching an under-21s match between Serbia and England, pelted a black English player with bananas. When the racist implication that the black man was a monkey was objected to, there was incredulity from the Serbian fascists at this thought; their joke was only a bit of fun. They said that those who had thought of the implied racism were the true racists, not those throwing bananas—furthermore, they had no sense of humour. In this case, the English team stood by and defended their comrade, and so he was not left alone; the desire to attack alterity and the true nature of the racists was thus revealed.

We can see that the behaviour of the group has a profound significance—that is, whether they join in the attack or stay quietly neutral, as if it is nothing to do with them, or whether a critical number stand up with the victim against the double attack. Racism, anti-Semitism, and homophobia do not work in an atmosphere in which the premises of the attack are strongly rejected. In such cases, the attackers come under scrutiny for the first time and cannot hide in the group. Nor can they pervert the group into identifying with them in their attack.

To consider another case, in Paris, January 2015, the murder of French journalists by Islamist terrorists, in response to their satirical depictions of Muhammad, and then two days later the killings of Jews, caused an eruption of outrage. In this aftermath, a sense of "us" vs "them" began to percolate through the drama. Rather than understanding that the attack was carried out by a small cell of terrorists motivated by contempt and hatred for French and Western society, this reaction allowed the attack to succeed in causing further splits between Muslim French citizens and how they were perceived by non-Muslim French citizens, as if all were capable of killing in the name of Allah. Instead of a group process that brought the country together, there was an increase in anti-Muslim sentiment.

Worse still was the opportunity taken by a few senior Israeli politicians to employ anti-Semitism as a device to demand that all French Jews quickly relocate to the safety of Israel. Here there is a further attack, this time on the French state that apparently cannot guard the lives of its Jewish citizens—the twisted assumption being that Israel is a safe place for Jews, something that has been clearly untrue all the way from the inception of the state in 1948 up to the present. According to the Israeli Prime Minister, Benjamin

Netanyahu, Europe, the terrible place that was the crucible of the Holocaust and that has harboured the continuation of anti-Semitism ever since, no longer deserves to have Jews living there.

In this example, the ripples through society and politics, and between nation states, pile on top of each other, allowing an attempt to gain advantage, following terrible wounds to individuals, communities, and countries, by suggesting that bystanders and citizens should take various sides. In such situations, thinking is necessary to avoid further layers of encrypted and potential trauma being doubled up and intensified—something that the abused child is much more vulnerable to doing.

Of course, we now have President Trump, with his crude stereotyping of the other and continual projections of destructiveness on to a person or people other than himself and his administration. The "alt-right", the Ku Klux Klan, and Nazi groups have consequently found their voices, empowered by the Trumpian dystopic vision and its profound capacity for lies. Trump's attacks, which encourage his supporters to further vilify individuals or groups, have the same structure as the double racist attack of the fascist Serbian football fans. Yet it seems that Trump has an additional capacity to mesmerise by taking a grossly oversimplified, untruthful position that is so off-centre that the listener has to continually rethink what is being said. This is a form of unbalancing the other, including his staff; he alone is above the fray, commenting from the heights of the presidency and invariably causing chaos, which in fact seems to be his goal. His deepening of the poverty of so many people, in a sea of riches for the few, is the recipe for an eruption of anger to be utilised, as in the 1930s, by a regime leaning towards totalitarianism.

Trump too often comments on a situation in which someone has identified and called out a situation, within a society or institution, as anti-other, stating that it is, in fact, that person who is the problem. "It is really your fault as you are the one who is bad since you accuse the other of racism, anti-Semitism, etc." If that person speaks up against Trump's smear, she or he is attacked further. This dynamic can be seen repeated time and time again, and it is partly a result of the identification that people can have with the group, institution, or tradition being criticised. For people who identify with a group as a good object, someone who points to problems of discrimination within it is turned into the problem. This is Trump's attack dog upping his accusatory rhetoric to blame Mexicans, Muslims, the poor, the pope, all of whom can be split off and contained behind a wall of separateness, us vs them, like an excretory process. We treat fellow human beings in the same way that we void shit and piss, getting rid of the "bad stuff" without guilt, as if they were "nothing". This was central to Hitler's Final Solution, the processes of which were oiled by its victims being cast as *Untermenschen*. In this particularly vicious psychology, in order for the many to feel "great again", some groups have to be demeaned and got rid of (in the 1930s, it was Communists, homosexuals, cripples, Gypsies, and Jews).

Remember that Holocaust Memorial Day in the US in 2018 had, for the first time, no mention of the Jews. It is important in cases such as this to understand the importance of words—their inclusions, elisions, and transformations. Similarly, the renaming of a political party is never something meaningless; the policies continuing in the same direction, only under a different name. In March 2018, the French right-wing Front National proposed changing its name to "Rassemblement National". There was already a centre-right party using this name and they issued a legal challenge attempting to block its use by Marine Le Pen's party. However, in the light of the extreme right-wing nature of the Front National, their wish to take the name "Rassemblement National" is particularly disturbing; a party who supported the Nazis operated with that name from 1941 to 1944, their flag and logo resembling the Nazi flag with its swastika. The Front National's attempt at rebranding thus appears to be a return of that which had been repressed.

Psychoanalysis and resisting domination

To speak up against developments such as these requires a certain bravery, whether acting alone or as part of a group, in order to deal with the anxiety of being out of step with the perceived majority. As Frank Kermode says in his famous essay *The Sense of an Ending*:

> This is not, after all, quite the world of those who seek 'the courage to be and strip reality of the protection of myth'.
>
> (Kermode, 2000, p. 132–133)

In analysis also, it is always a continuing struggle for the analysand to find that state of being that is distinct from immersion in his or her primary narrative. Analysis can be an act of freedom against the chains of imposed and self-imposed narratives from family history or unconscious romance, but it also has to struggle against the passive expectation that something will be done by someone else, often expressing itself as the desire for this to be the analyst's function. One of the main themes examined in this chapter is how central these issues of freedom and emancipation are to the analytic process. This centrality is the reason for the explosion of analytic training subsequent to the tearing down of the Berlin Wall (another wall built to separate people), the freedom that came with the collapse of Communism leading many who had lived under its corrupting ideology to desire an analytic treatment—one that would allow them an interior space in the mind in which they could examine the mental damage accrued from living in a paranoid culture. The deep fear for these individuals was their own mental corruption and complicity. Who informed on me and how can I alleviate my guilt for having informed? How can I rebalance my mind to restore my parents' authority, rather than the state's? The need is to purge the poison in the individual's unconscious state of mind after being sur-rounded by non-stop brainwashing, divested of the capacity to think for themselves. Privacy, confidentiality, and the development of trust became essential tools for many who thus came to appreciate the huge value of psychoanalytic holding, as well as analytic investigation into the impact on citizens of massive state corruption. The developed capacity to mourn such external and internal traumatic states, through nurturing the capacity to free associate, provided minds with the freedom to think. Free association is not just a profound technique advanced by Freud; it is also a formation of mind that is central to developing societies and politics that are creative and free.

This is particularly important in our world today with the recent and continuing global financial crisis exposing the hidden world of selfishness. The other side to the accumulation of great wealth is the severe deprivation of so much of the population. The poor are then blamed as if their poverty is their own fault. Again, the double attack. You are poor—unlike us—and it is your fault. There is always a necessity to find an object to blame, and, in addition to the poor, this can just as easily be blacks, Muslims, or always the ubiquitous Jew. As many European societies shift further to the right, and human values seemingly become polarised into primitive dichotomies of us vs them, the spectre of totalitarianism returns to haunt us all. More than ever, an analytic thinking space is necessary as one form of resisting the lurch into domination, both in society and in family life.

Time and the ending

The timelessness of an analysis also lives in the time that it contains and examines. An analysis is about a beginning, a middle, and an ending. The end is ever-present in the living of our lives, both for the individual and for society, as well as for a particular analysis. Death is a certainty of the condition of being alive, even if for many it remains unknown to consciousness. This needs to be part of any analysis—the imagined deaths of the analyst and of the analysand, and the fusion of these two strands in the end of the treatment. We die and will be in the minds of those we leave behind; similarly, the end of an analysis leaves both parts of the dyad to have in mind, from time to time, "remembrances of things past". The individual runs mythically from moment to moment, while our culture runs in grander aliquots from year to year, across the century, or to the pull of the millennium. In 2010, the International Psychoanalytical Association (IPA) commemorated its centenary, as if the survival of psychoanalysis (and not its often-longed-for death) is contingent upon the magic of reaching 100 years of age (this not incompatible with the idea that psychoanalysis, as a discipline, a *mere* hundred years old, is still a child or adolescent).

It is interesting here to consider Kermode's contrasting of long spans of time, such as centuries, with the insistent ticking of the clock that pulls us along our journey from birth to death. He describes the commencing movement in the sound of "tick" as a humble genesis to the more guttural sound of "tock", a type of feeble apocalypse—the pause being the life in between. In contrast to this narrative structure, with its formulaic direction from then until now, Kermode suggests that we might instead hear the sequence differently, as "tock–tick" (Kermode 2000, p. 45). In this tiny metaphor, Kermode breaks through into dissonance, inviting us to view the seemingly well-ordered sequence as a potentially fractured noise. The "tock" is a more dissonant sound, and so by reversing the sequence, to "tock–tick", that dissonance becomes more prominent, and this reversal is also jarring through its distortion of the familiar order.

Of course, a person's life can be conceptualised in terms of a forward-moving dynamic. Yet, if we are to think about the structure of beginning and ending, and insert the "tock" first, the time interval, despite being the same, carries a very different resonance. It contains dissonance, which is the stuff our patients bring to us when the clock needs resetting, in their perceptions of the dominance of dissonant rhythms in their lives. Tick–tock is a human narrative created to fill the void of time as the clock moves ever forward. However, psychoanalysis has a freedom to mentally escape such shackles and to go backwards when necessary, hearing "tock–tick", in order to re-find lost objects or the history of the patient. This is the value too of *après coup*, or *Nachträglichkeit*, which allows the possibility of going back in time and unconsciously re-evaluating etchings on the mind.

Re-finding lost objects is of course in itself another mythical quest, but it is one in which there can be a rebalancing of what can feel like the magical drive of destiny, such that the individual may realise more responsibility for his or her own causality. This means escaping the groove of a slavish, unconscious drive to continue the life one has grown up with, including its perceptions, misperceptions, and prejudices, as if our character and object relationships have been fixed by the contingencies of life as something concrete that cannot, must not, be altered. Beneath such phantasies that things are fixed for all time resides the fear of "and then what?" What might the individual do with their trauma within a skein of severe disturbances in society, such as totalitarianism, where political lying and attacks on alterity develop a pseudo-normality? What is to be made of life in the empty space without the patch that seems to hold it all together? This is a place where psychoanalytic dialogue can be formative, allowing the concrete patch to be prised away so that a new healing can begin. The free-associative thinking that allows this process can contribute a new dialogue, and a new way to think about political discourse, in doing so opening up the freedom to have an adventure, to be alive in one's life—to think and to be in society—even as the long shadow descends into the dark.

Thinking on the border
memory and trauma in society

I remember very strongly in the days after, sitting and looking for a word or a metaphor or something like that, and then I suddenly ask myself: "Am I an idiot?" All around me the world has collapsed and I am looking for a word. And then when I found the right word there was this feeling that I had done something right in a world that had turned out to be totally wrong. In a world that was then a big mistake for me, I was finding the thread of a story again, and was able to imagine, even, or to fantasise, and to infuse my characters with love and humour and passion. After a while I understood writing is a way to act against the gravity of sadness, of grief, and to choose life in the end of it.
—David Grossman talking about the *shivah* for his son (2012)

How does an individual return from the far reaches of certain terrible experiences? From being in the trenches of the Somme? From crawling through the sewers of the Warsaw Ghetto? From being in the cities bombed to oblivion—Dresden, Coventry, Nagasaki, Hiroshima? From the many bombings and attacks around the world today, provoking huge numbers of people to try to escape violence and death by fleeing to Europe—and to risk death by doing so? And from the severe subsequent rise in anti-immigrant rhetoric, and in prejudice towards others?

25

In his essay "Experience and Poverty", Walter Benjamin writes that experience was traditionally transferred through stories and proverbs from one generation to the next, but that the incommunicably tragic atrocities of the First World War had interrupted this process, making it impossible (Benjamin, 1933, p. 731). As summarised by the editors of *The Storyteller*, a collection of Benjamin's short fiction:

> With the war came the severing of "the red thread of experience" which had connected previous generations, as Benjamin puts it in "Sketched into Mobile Dust". The "fragile human body" that emerged from the trenches was mute, unable to narrate the "forcefield of destructive torrents and explosions" that had engulfed it … It was as if the good and bountiful soil of the fable had become the sticky and destructive mud of the trenches, which would bear no fruit but only moulder as a graveyard.
>
> (Dolbear, Leslie, & Truskolaski, 2016, p. xi)

As with the war that Benjamin is reflecting on, it seems that experiences of massive destruction are always too much for us to bear really knowing and understanding. Our minds can only take in a certain amount of horror. So what becomes of the rest of the experience, which we resist? Those who knew from experience the horrors of the Somme could not tell its stories. The friends, body parts, insanities, the enemy… The reasons were all muddied up and coloured darkly. Detail had to be kept for the realms of the private nightmare, and not for telling others.

Other than our family members and close friends, most of us do not witness the dying and the dead. Seeing the dying and the dead in massive numbers overwhelms the human mind. For centuries, states have been adept at instigating and manipulating ideal qualities that they desire their citizens to have, as well as projecting negative qualities onto the other. The virulent propaganda in both directions demanded that each side of the 1914–1918 conflict believe that God was on their side, and not the other's. After the conflict ended, the millions of soldiers returned in silence, bringing back home their war despair.

Later, towards the end of the Second World War, Winston Churchill was clear that the concentration camps had to be filmed in order for the world to believe they had existed. Alfred Hitchcock gave guidance on the project, advising on long panning shots that would indicate the absence of manipulation and so the clear veracity of the scenes. The anxiety was that they would be accused of having made a filmic Hollywood story—one that could not really have happened. And so the filmmakers strove to secure the truth of the terrible scenes as the local town burghers visited, watching as the remaining SS guards, forced by British soldiers, buried the vast numbers of corpses. Supposedly, these burghers had been unaware of what had been happening just a few miles from their satisfied town lives—since demonstrated to be a lie (see Goldhagen, 1996). Incredibly, the film was immediately suppressed and has only recently been digitalised by the Imperial War Museum. On general release in 2015, some 70 years later, is a documentary of both its making and suppression called *Night Will Fall* (*Guardian* 9 Jan 2015). Politics had seemingly no time for knowledge and mourning. Better to get on with the political tasks of the imminent Cold War. Knowledge and truth are overridden by the politics of the day.

We see similar behaviour in the Nazi denial of the Holocaust and the post-war political desire to avoid knowledge of it. In Poland, the paradoxically named Law and Justice party, in power since 2015, recently sent a law to be signed by Andrzej Duda, the Polish president, that criminalises any assertion of Polish participation in the Holocaust or other war crimes occurring under the German occupation of the country (Shore, 2018). Duda soon complied and signed the bill, under pressure from both the party and rallies of protesters outside his presidential palace. Meanwhile, the world receives Trump's daily tweets, denying truth and attacking the press. Mirroring the situation in Poland, the American president's attacks appear to be an early staging post for a potential modern-day dictator, striving for total state control.

In medieval times, when most villagers never went more than a few miles beyond their habitations and fields, it was true that what was a little further beyond was unknown. Such territory was imagined to be as it was told in fables: strange lands of giants, warriors, and dangerous sirens. Today, however, what used to be imagined is no longer imagined. The question is, what has this done to the human mind, our collective narratives about the world—acting as our unconscious, imaginative frame—perhaps no longer able to hold the immensity of the violent images within it? And if such images are beyond the strength of our minds, what is the consequent impact on our values and character formations? Are we becoming hardened in our relations with the other, drawn to destructiveness, aggression, sadomasochism?

It is easier, for many people, who do not want to find a place for such things in their minds, to avoid all knowledge of them—and here we must reference the unconscious states of denial and disavowal—resulting in severe unconscious splitting and a general contempt for knowledge in such areas. The recent political cry, therefore, that experts have no value, can also be understood in this context. Psychoanalytic thought asserts that horrid things that are known can become encrypted, almost lost (Abraham & Torok, 1994, pp. 162–164), this forming the core of the dynamic of severe individual trauma in the child (see Ferenczi, 1933). If no adult sees the attacks on the body and mind of the abused child, such denial develops, in the developing mind of the victim, into a lasting capacity to not see. Perhaps, in today's world, the banal concept of "mindfulness" has at its root the commonality of mindlessness (the assertion of the antonym does not restore that which must not be seen and felt). As in Bluebeard's castle, in which the murdered wives are locked away, hidden knowledge is only an invitation to continue perverse functioning. The petrification of the writhing bodies in Pompeii, at the moment of the volcanic eruption, provides us with a vivid metaphor for the rigidity and fixity of the mind following massive traumas. Better stay fixed, rigid, and without sight; the scenes are too much for humankind to bear.

But let us go more slowly. Myths, legends, and stories have perhaps been idealised precisely because they have, over the centuries, been changed and developed so that they are acceptable to grown-ups and their children. The original Grimm brothers' fairy tales, for example, were published in December 1812, with further, increasingly milder revisions being regularly published up until the final edition in 1857 (Flood, 2014). There had been no English translation of the original edition until Jack Zipes' in 2014. The original tales were changed significantly in the later editions that were used for the previous translations. For instance, in the original "How the Children Played at Slaughtering", the children play a game in which one is a butcher and the others are pigs. It ends with a boy cutting his brother's throat, and then being stabbed by his mother in fury. The child that she had left alone in the bath drowns, and the returning father, overwhelmed by despondency, soon dies. In the children's fairy story, the normative reality that families sustain life is challenged to a mythic extreme as family violence erupts. In a similarly less-sanitised original, Rapunzel, following a "merry time" with the prince, and unaware of the biological consequences, exclaims, "Tell me, Mother Gothel, why are my clothes becoming too tight?" "Letting down one's hair" may be a metaphor for sex in the tower; a subject of much interest to children in their quest to discover where babies come from. The original stories clearly observe and speak much more directly to the unconscious—so much so that six editions of revisions were necessary to turn them safely into children's classics (ibid.).

***

From the classics to soundbites. In today's world, the impact of journalism has been softened through its transformation into soundbites—easily digested bites of information that gesture towards a particular matter without going into the detail that might (and ought to) disturb the reader, who thus easily and swiftly passes on to the next item. News is presented in rapid compilations so that each story has a similar valence. We are enabled in scanning over them, moving quickly past potential disturbances to our emotional life in the quest to be superficially up-to-date with everything that is happening.

Meanwhile, the 968 million users of Facebook are asked each day to share their thoughts and feelings. As Katrina Forrester describes, these users are prompted to choose from a list of options, inputting data which is then put to disconcerting uses:

> "Excited" is the first option, "happy" is the second. If they don't fit, you can scroll down through 120 other moods. ... In 2014, we learned that [Facebook] gathers [this] data about our moods, and ran experiments in manipulating [its users' moods] by tailoring newsfeeds to be more happy or more sad.
>
> (Forrester, 2015)

This is a business model in which huge numbers of people are each fed a different, personalised news diet based on what they appear to like in order to manipulate their thinking. The social media monolith profits from "making what goes on in our heads knowable, legible, and marketable" (ibid.), and this means we are only shown the news that our supplier knows will engage our emotional life, filtered rather than raw, and so maximise our engagement with their platform.

On top of this, we have now entered what has been labelled a "post-truth" world, where significant streams of information and news have a willingly non-existent relationship with truth and evidence. Google's algorithms recently reflected the scale of this phenomenon, and the amount of material online that denies the Holocaust, by briefly declaring that the Holocaust was a fake. The tick-box ease of this twenty-first-century environment ensures that we think less. In this anodyne state, we become increasingly vulnerable to the manipulations of news moguls and unscrupulous politicians. Complicit with our own surveillance, we reveal so many of our habits, likes, and dislikes to the market via our laptops and smartphones, living in this state as though it is only our momentary happiness that matters, and as though we no longer require a mental organisation with the capacity to think.

A Trump rally shows the power of pleasing the people who exist in this state with barely concealed racism, misogyny, and anti-Semitism, rousing them with the slogan "Make America Great Again". Of course, Europe has known this script well, Hitler reading from it at the Nuremberg rallies. We know the consequences that can occur when the people give up thinking, basking in the idealisation of the leader and his influences. Like the ease of soundbites and clicking "yes" or "no", the political process is diverted away from thought and into the black-and-white simplicity of splitting *us* from *them*. And the people are very happy.

Modern psychiatry has its own complicity in this elision of thought. The latest *Diagnostic and Statistical Manual of Mental Disorders*, for example, classes grief following a bereavement, if it lasts for longer than a couple of months, as a mental disorder (American Psychiatric Association, 2013). And so Big Pharma sells more antidepressants. More insidious than such profit-chasing, however, is a new mythology that nothing should move us away from our happy state. In this mindset, mourning is one of the processes that is seen to be antithetical to the individual's well-being. Against this unsettling trend, we must hold firmly to our knowledge that a remembering of the other, as well as our own individual histories, within the context of our complex emotional and relational lives, is what enables us to be alive in a process of thinking for ourselves. Totalitarian states hate psychoanalysis as it wakes the sleeping people from the anti-democratic manipulations of mass psychology. As mentioned in the previous chapter, since the fall of the Berlin Wall, there has been a flourishing of psychoanalysis in Eastern Europe, helping to end one such slumber.

Jan Kizilhan and the Yazidi: therapy and justice after genocide

Let us now return, by telling another story, to discussion of matters that are impossible to discuss. On 15 August 2014, the headline of the German newspaper *Bild* was "*Isis betreiben Genozid auf Raten*" ("Step by step, Isis carries out genocide") (Kizilhan, 2014). It followed the capture by Isis of the city of Sinjar in northern Iraq and described the atrocities the group had been inflicting on the local Yazidi community: enslavement, torture, executions, and a systematic programme of rape—victims of which were as young as eight (Sands, 2016). Philippe Sands, who interviewed Jan Kizilhan, the author of the article—a German psychologist and also, himself, a Yazidi Kurd—relates that he used the word "genocide" both because it was accurate and in order to motivate action. The psychologist was soon at the centre of a project to rescue 1,100 Yazidi women and girls and bring them to Germany, where they would be safe and would receive medical treatment (ibid.). In Sinjar, Isis had given the Yazidi the choice of either converting to Islam or being executed. Some 50,000 were forced to the surrounding mountains, where they starved (ibid.).

The Yazidi community, numbering less than one million, believe in a god who is both good and bad, and worship the peacock angel. The peacock angel was the first to descend from their god to earth, shedding its colourful feathers. For Isis, however, the angel is a representation only of the devil, and they call the Yazidi "devil worshippers". Either they convert to Islam or are killed, with no other possibility (ibid.). This is a world of only black and white: no peacock colours, no room for debate and no space to be alive.[1]

Kizilhan visited refugee camps in northern Iraq to assess who to bring back to Germany. The criteria were: "Had the woman or girl escaped from Isis captivity? Was there clear evidence of severe abuse and psychological consequences from the period of captivity? Would treatment in Germany help, beyond what was available locally?" (ibid.). He conducted 1,403 interviews, most of which were 30 minutes, although some took up to two hours. Kizilhan describes the severe stress involved:

> It was hell to make such decisions, to decide for that one, yes, … but for another one, no. … The youngest person I examined was eight years old. … She was sold eight times, raped more than 100 times over a period of 14 months. … That case was clear, she came because otherwise she would not survive.
> (Kizilhan, interviewed in Sands, 2016)

Kizilhan's selection of who to bring back to Germany for treatment eerily echoes the murderous Selektion in the concentration camps. In this case, however, victims are selected for therapeutic treatment as part of an offer of a new life. This runs in parallel to Angela Merkel's decision to allow over one million refugees to claim asylum in Germany in 2015 (Mohdin, 2017). These visionary projects embody the opposite of Nazism's murdering of millions. They incense Germany's alt-right and neo-Nazis, their hatred smouldering.

Another girl was a zombie-like sixteen-year-old, who had been held captive for two weeks before escaping. Isis had raped her sister, and so, to protect herself, she chose to make herself unattractive: she poured oil over herself and burnt 80 per cent of her body. She has since undergone twelve operations (Sands, 2016). "When I asked her what she would like most, she said she'd like to be able to walk down a street, sit in a café, have an ice-cream, without anyone staring at her" (Kizilhan, interviewed in Sands, 2016).

One 26-year-old woman who was taken to Germany, took her two children with her, five and six years old. She used to have three children. After Isis executed 21 men from her family in front of them, including her husband and her father, she was sold repeatedly, and raped. The last man she was sold to was a foreign fighter called Abu Jihat. He made her learn the Koran. Then, as her Arabic was not good enough, he punished her. He shut her daughter, Tuli, who was two years old, in a tin box outside in the courtyard—in the heat of Raqqa in August—and said to the mother, "If you take her out, I will [kill] the other two children." He left her there for seven days, after which he took her out, submerged her in ice-cold water, beat her, and broke her back. She died after two days. Abu Jihat told the mother, "This is how the unbelievers will be treated" (ibid.). Kizilhan has difficulty understanding such horror and inhumanity and can explain it only by assuming that Isis turn their victims into non-humans, in the same way the Nazis did (ibid.).

In Germany, the women and girls are put into groups of about twenty and seen weekly for individual psychotherapy, as well as receiving group therapy. There has been a large amount of voluntary support from the community in Königsfeld, as well as beyond. The victims will stay in Germany, yet whatever help they are given there is also a need for justice, in order to be able to hope (ibid.). Tuli's mother, for example, wants the details of her daughter's death to be known widely, and she wants the murderer to be punished. Similarly, one seventeen-year-old woman states that "My sister and brother were beheaded in my presence. … Daesh [Isis] has to be destroyed" (Sands, 2016). German prosecutors are investigating these crimes. It is sad that, although the Nazi war criminals are now virtually all dead, a new generation has experienced genocide. It is appropriate that German authorities are active in bringing justice to the Yazidi.

From witnessing impacts of genocide, the necessary component, in addition to the individual's treatment, is to bring the perpetrators to justice: the monster must be locked up for the victim to have a better chance of being able to sleep. Importantly, it also means that the victim does not need to continue being the one who is unconsciously punished. Justice can, on a deep level of the mind, mitigate the masochism that the vicious and sadistic object demands; as if there has to be a fixed, binary pairing of sadist and masochist, always linking the oppressor and the victim. This is the same dynamic as paedophilia, where the perpetrator says to the child, "You like it really," even, "You made me do it to you," and, "It is your fault," potentially setting the child on a lifetime of masochistic behaviour. What can we do with this modern-day horror story, other than ask how it is possible, and thus attempt to trace its history?

Confronting the past in the present

We need to move from our more superficial states of knowledge about the world around us to hear and feel whatever comes to mind from specific histories, whether recent or further into the past. The Jews of Lublin, one third of its population, were wiped out in the Second World War in Majdanek, the extermination camp on the outskirts of the city. Forty-three thousand Jews were murdered, leaving just three hundred survivors. Today, there is a cultural institute in Lublin—Grodzka Gate NN Theatre—which is dedicated to documenting the lives of those who were killed. It takes its name from its location in the Grodzka Gate, which for centuries divided the Christian part of the city from the Jewish part.

In an article on the uncovering of the city's previously hidden history, Henry Foy (2015) describes that a huge car park is visible from the gate, beneath which the post-war Communist authorities buried the old Jewish quarter. The foundations of houses that belonged to the murdered Jews still exist beneath the tarmac veneer. Interviewed for the article, the founder of Grodska Gate NN Theatre, Tomasz Pietrasiewicz, says that, "despite this concrete shell, the memories come through. … This is not only the disclosure of a forgotten town but it is a reaction to something that is still a moral issue, saving the memory of what happened here." As Foy relates, the Communist regime in Poland began, in the late 1960s, a vicious anti-Semitic campaign, driving away many of the Jews who had survived and causing a dearth of documentary evidence in the city's library and museum relating to the Jewish population that had been exterminated. And so, in the 1990s, Pietrasiewicz began gathering stories, partial memories, photographs, letters, and diaries. (We can see a similarity here with the fragmentary process of analysis, collecting pieces of material that have been buried beneath our individual "tarmac".) So far, the institute has established a file for 900 of the 1,500 homes that once stood in Jewish Lublin, each filled with photographs and documents relating to the people who lived in them. For the next stage, which will be even more challenging, the researchers will begin a file for each of the residents who lived in the city before the Holocaust.

This work is described by Pietrasiewicz as "creating an ark of memory to take into the future" (ibid.). Foy describes a particularly poignant room in the artistic installation within the institute, a dark, foreboding space with many tree trunks, that represents the legend of the arrival of Jews in Poland: "[they found] a forest outside Lublin with trees marked with the word 'Polin', Hebrew for 'you should stay here'[; thus] Polin became the Hebrew word for Poland." As Pietrasiewicz says, "What the Nazis wanted to do was not only kill the Jews but erase any trace of them afterwards" (ibid.)—an aim in pursuit of which the anti-Semitic Polish Communists led and encouraged their citizens.

Pietrasiewicz's project is one that strives to confront a dark absence by searching for names and stories in the huge task of building the archive. This is a painful, lengthy, emotional struggle embarked on in an attempt to rescue a forgotten history. It goes far beyond the current prevalent mindset in which we chase only our promised quotient of happiness. Lublin can be a beacon of memory and a memorial looking back to the past, at the same time educating the present community by asking, "How is this story possible?"

Let us open the lens up again so that we can consider the present and the massive wave of immigration that has rocked the EU. The German government supports Kizilhan's humanitarian initiative. However, in Germany, and throughout the continent, there has been a huge surge in anti-immigrant and racist sentiment and behaviour. One tool at our disposal for combatting this increase is to describe in detail the murder and torture both inflicted historically and still being inflicted today. This cannot be communicated through soundbites, which allow the listener to avoid feelings about ongoing atrocities. Nor can the detail be a means to invite a sadistic pleasure of "it's them rather than me". Rather, the detail should invite the listener to remember and to assert "never again", enabling them to resist the insidious aggression of taking sides between us and them.

These assertions must also include the consideration of the longer-term impact of severe trauma on its survivors within society. In June 1986, *Shoah*—Claude Lanzmann's epic documentary about the Holocaust released in April 1985—was screened in Israel for the first time. One arresting sentence in the film comes in an interview with Yithak "Antek" Zuckerman, who for years had been celebrated in Israel for his role in leading the uprising in the Warsaw Ghetto. After telling Lanzmann that he had started drinking after the war, Antek says, "It was very difficult. Claude, you asked for my impression. If you could lick my heart, it would poison you" (Lanzmann, 1985). As Lanzmann tells Jonathan Freedland (2015), the kibbutzniks tried hard to prevent him from meeting Antek, "because they were so ashamed of him … [They] did not want to show a hero who drinks." Lanzmann succeeded, however, and so, when he screened the film in Israel, he was able to confront Israelis with the uncomfortable insight that those who had been lionised for their resistance had in fact been broken by their traumatic experiences. As Freedland notes, Lanzmann also,

> by letting his camera linger so long on Poland and Poles—to an extent still resented by many in that country—succeeded in shifting the focus from Germany alone. *Shoah* made clear that the elimination of the Jews was not only a German project, but involved most of the nations of Europe.
>
> (ibid.)

If we acknowledge that most of the nations of Europe were involved in the elimination of Jews, it becomes necessary to also consider the actions of the Allied countries. We should consider, for example, that the Allies thought about but refused to bomb Auschwitz. Wagner's mansion in Bayreuth had been precision bombed, leaving his opera house, just a few hundred metres away, intact, and so it would certainly have been possible to safely bomb the concentration camp. However, the debate at the time was suffused with doubt and the fear of killing Jews (before the full extent of the Nazi killing machine had been understood). The Jewish Agency eventually appealed to Churchill, who told his foreign secretary, Anthony Eden, "to get anything out of the Air Force you can and invoke me if necessary" (Berenbaum, 2001). Yet the RAF still did not bomb Auschwitz. The IG Farben plant less than eight kilometres east of Birkenau, which manufactured oil for Germany, was a priority for the US, and was bombed in August 1944, but Birkenau was still left untouched (ibid.). It seems possible, then, that this decision not to bomb the camps might have had anti-Semitic motivations. On the other hand, it might just be an example of the profound complexity of the war, and due rather to concerns about the possibility of Jews being killed in any such bombings.

It is crucial to acknowledge that the Holocaust is not confined in archival footage to the past: it is all around us, present in the here and now. The place in which it occurred is not some distant world, a mythical planet called Auschwitz. It happened in this place and this town and this field, as attested to by the project of remembrance and revival in the city of Lublin. In describing these matters, saying how this and this and that are possible, we bring various fragments of history to the surface. This history exists now, in this moment while you are reading this book.

We must adopt a similarly assertive mentality when faced with the current problems of the hate of the other, released in Europe by the British Brexit votes and in the US by vicious Trumpian statements, allowing and inviting hate talk to be perceived as normal speech. This is our present world and as psychoanalysts it is crucial that we speak out wherever there is reprehensible speech around us, in our countries and our cities, with our friends if necessary, and even with some of our colleagues. To turn a blind eye is a passive acquiescence to the cruel scenes. After all, the dynamics of sadomasochism and hate of the object are well known to us, both in our theories and in our living of the transference and countertransference in our consulting rooms.

Freud lived through the end of the First World War and witnessed the rise of the Nazis. Yet he was unable to speak against the political times in which he lived; psychoanalysis needed to be preserved, and perhaps it was too much of a risk, both for him and for the preservation of his legacy. He was certainly fearful that psychoanalysis would be seen as a Jewish science, which would mark it as a target for the Nazis, just as his books had been in 1933. But in today's bitter times, it cannot be right that psychoanalysts have nothing to say. As a subject that studies pathology, cruelties, and severe states of mind, psychoanalysis has the perceptual tools to help communities and even politicians to a deeper understanding of the violence within society, and thus to help us stand our ground against the pull to vilify and blame the other, split off our disturbing characteristics or possible causes for instability or deprivation, and relieve ourselves of blame or concern.[2]

It is time for our profession, in addition to listening to and talking with our analysands, to speak to society—to describe some of the small human fragments in the events happening around us, and to give witness to the depth of pain within them. Descriptions of the states of mind found in the analyses of the individual, especially in relation to trauma, can be applied to the states of conflict, splitting, and sadomasochism that lurk on the fringes of society awaiting their call. It is time to break the cycle of deadly mimetic violence by refusing to mirror our enemies. By that, I mean that we need to adopt a hard-nosed defiance rather than a sense that nothing can be done except to watch passively. And, in order to resist the pull to stand aside, we need to know more of our own unconsciously destructive and racist states of mind.

Mourning, melancholia, and *ubuntu*

I would like to touch on the South African concept of *ubuntu*. In Desmond Tutu's words, this is the idea that:

> [one person's] humanity is caught up, is inextricably bound up, in [another's]. ... "A person is a person through other people." ... A person with *ubuntu* ... has a proper self-assurance that comes from knowing that he or she belongs in a greater whole and is diminished when others are humiliated or diminished, when others are tortured or oppressed.
>
> (Tutu, 1999, pp. 34–36)

We are part of the social problem if we take the easy solution of locating/projecting the blame on to the other, and if we do not realise that our securing of ourselves from the other, the immigrant, is a reflection of fragments of our intrinsic hostility towards otherness. We are all racist, anti-Semitic characters who, in our unconscious, want to murder our siblings. If we remain children, this only unconsciously confirms the power of our destructiveness. The mature position of *ubuntu*, in contrast to this, is a difficult place to reach. Yet, as the defining atmosphere of the Truth and Reconciliation Commission in South Africa, it allowed mourning, albeit with an often-forced closure of trauma.

I would like to further open up the concept of mourning by examining its difference from melancholia. Mourning takes place when the object that has been lost was loved for its own sake, the individual being capable of empathy—of understanding the feeling of another. To achieve mourning, and a mourning in which the subject retains their self-esteem, everything that is attached to the lost object has to be thought about, a reconciliation found with its loss: this is known as the work of mourning. By contrast, loss that gives rise to melancholia is due to a narcissistic choice, the vanished object having been loved in the individual's own image, adapted to their unconscious phantasy. As the subject's self-esteem depended in part on the lost object, they are left bereft of part of themselves. As Margarete and Alexander Mitscherlich wrote:

> This applied perfectly to the Führer; he fulfilled the ideal of greatness for his subjects, who had long been crippled by absolutism and, in turn, projected *his* ideas of greatness onto the "race" which supposedly gave distinction to the German people. By doing so, Adolf Hitler could entertain the thought that not he himself was responsible for his downfall, but that the German people had proven unworthy of him.
>
> (Mitscherlich & Mitscherlich, 1967, p. 28)

For the Mitscherlichs, the Germans' collective denial of the past was expressed for many years in the manic energy with which the ruins were cleared away and the economy rebuilt, tasks which were not about mourning but rather rebuilding a national facade. This was aided in West Germany by the Allies, helping to re-build and strengthen it against any encroachments from East Germany and Russia, while East Germany was similarly aided by Russia, bolstering it against the West. The Cold War thus dominated politics, split off from any concern for the lack of mourning for the massive war crimes that had been committed, and the reality of the Third Reich became distanced from the present, upstaged by the popularity of building new structures.

In this way, the mind of Germany, now split into two parts, forewent its memories of the vicious, perverse crimes that had been committed, avoiding all mourning as if such a complete bypassing of the remembrance of recent times could be normal. As the Mitscherlichs note, it was only "pressure of opinion outside Germany [that] forced Germans to institute legal proceedings against Nazi criminals, to extend the statute of limitations, and to reconstruct the circumstances of mass crimes" (ibid., p. 29). However, this superficial blanket withdrawal from the crimes of the Third Reich did not mean that the Third Reich was not still present in an internal delusional world. The Communist devouring of East Germany had been what

Hitler had been guarding from happening, and this had now taken place as a result of the actions of the Allies, together with the still-prevalent phantasy of a Jewish Bolshevik plot. There is a clear sense of continuity between this us vs them mentality of the Third Reich and the energy that each side of Germany, East and West, employed in rebuilding and defending against the other. This work was intended to defend each side from the other, and so both, paranoid with each other, had few thoughts about the underlying horrors of the concentration camps. They passed the time in this way, as if through so doing the past would be dealt with, its contents covered over. Many similarities can be seen between such systems of "us vs them" and the current easy language of "making America great again". In the same way that Hitler did, it is likely that, when Trump eventually falls, he will blame the people and shout his innocence.

Gaps, splits, and patches

In the context of hate towards the other within society, I now want to explore the possibility that an unconscious realisation of an emptiness at the heart of the state leads to a fear and rage about who or what might fill it. The leader, the king or queen, has been regarded since medieval times as having a double embodiment, his or her own body along with that of the state, this idea being based on the sacrifice of Christ's body for the world. In the Germany of 1945, therefore, Hitler's suicide, and the disappearance of his body (which was stolen by the Russians), left a psychic empty space, the utter devastation of Germany's cities of rubble reflecting the collapse of the German people's belief in their Führer. Similarly, when a king or queen is beheaded, whatever relief there might be on the part of revolutionaries is matched by fear around how the gap will be filled.

In 1989, with the fall of the Berlin Wall and the dissolution of the Eastern Bloc, we can note the thoughtful development of a psychic gap. In the context of this gap, the architecture of the rebuilt Reichstag can be seen as a symbol of the unified Germany, coming together, as it were, to repair the gap left by the previous wrenching of East Germany away from the whole and into totalitarianism. It is as if the separation between West and East Germany became gradually and painfully walled up, this becoming an applied patch such that reunification, in all of its complexities, could either conceal or begin to reveal the pain buried beneath the physical structures of the city. It is not surprising that, in strained times, the pull to return to a totalitarian world, and to lay blame on certain citizens, reappears as a haunting, demanding that the patch be reprised and strengthened rather than prised away. Yet this haunting also allows the possibility of what Michael Balint called a new beginning, enabling us to see, hear, feel, and examine repressed hatreds and cruelties as part of the work of mourning in which a new, creative direction can emerge.

There is a problem, though, regarding the meaning of a gap. How deep might a gap in the unconsciousness of a society be, or how deep might it become? Is healing taking place or are there deep cracks just beneath the surface, the remains, perhaps, of a Jewish ghetto beneath the tarmac of a carpark? In my earlier book, *Landscapes of the Dark*, I discuss this subject as follows:

> Freud's paper *Neurosis and Psychosis* (1924) is seminal for the way it allows us to understand not just the notion of a gap in the ego, but the struggle by the unconscious to make good the gap and to attempt repair: "In regard to the genesis of delusions", writes Freud, "a fair number of analyses have taught us that the delusion is found applied like a patch over the place where originally a rent had appeared in the ego's relation to the external world" (Freud 1924, p. 151). The gap, in time, can become the "split" in the ego. However, this is more complicated than it seems, as the German for "split" is *Einreiss*, which leans more to a meaning of a "tendency to tear". This throws another perspective on to Freud's meaning because a "tendency" includes the idea that despite being fragile, the tear may not worsen. It is not a break. This is less critical than a *Reiss*, which is an actual tear and is more a term to delegate to psychosis (Danckwardt & Wegner, 2007, p. 1118). This is the first recognition by Freud that the ego itself can be ill rather than healthy, being unable to stave off the other agencies of the mind. The split in the ego can mean that things are both really known and quite unknown simultaneously, like a life lived in a concurrent parallel way. Intellectually, one might prefer to think that if a person knows one and the other in parallel, then both states are known and the one knows the other, as it were. In severe mental illness, this is often not at all true. In addition, a sense of persecution from the tear in the mind can exist beneath the patch which is designed to cover it up. An *Einreiss* moving to a *Reiss* really does mean a deep gap between a mind knowing things on one side of the

canyon but hardly, if at all, beyond on the other side. The patch covering the tear in the mind like a dream is a symptom that attempts reconnection with reality. That *"which we take to be the pathological product, is in reality an attempt at recovery, a process of reconstruction"* writes Freud (1911, p. 71, italics in original).

(Sklar, 2011, pp. 8–9)

In terms of our societies, we can see such tears and patches in the deep and persistent paranoid hatreds of the other, gathering as historical emblems of us and them. Mass immigration into Europe and the US, the aftershocks of wars in Iraq, Syria, and Afghanistan, might have again roused those fears, many in receiving populations soon developing paranoid phantasies of themselves being evicted by the refugees. Societies become fractured with hatred as these ancient tropes rise from beneath the surface.

To consider another gap in a European context—that following the overthrow of Ceauşescu in Romania—we can turn to Slavoj Žižek's incisive reading:

> The rebels waving the national flag with the red star, the Communist symbol, cut out, so that instead of the symbol, standing for the organising principle of the national life, there was nothing but a hole in its center … The masses who poured into the streets of Bucharest "experienced" the situation as "open" … They participated in the unique intermediate state of passage from one discourse … to another, when, for a brief, passing moment, the hole in the big Other, the symbolic order, became visible.
>
> (Žižek, 1993, p. 1)

The symbolism described here is powerful, the empty space in the middle of the flag clearly representing the old Communist regime that had been dominated by Ceauşescu. Without the dreaded middle that was state control and oppression, the people were able to imagine a new idea of government, one symbolised with a newly found, "empty" flag. A people's uprising can thus force a massive shock into a corrupt society.

We can trace a similar perception of gaps in the present tumultuous reactions to massive migration into the EU, unconscious phantasies arising around the imagined meaning of the movement of outsiders into spaces existing or found all over the continent, disturbing the order. In these phantasies, it is as if there are newly found gaps being filled not by their leaders but by large groups of people from outside. Perhaps it is just this much-reported spectacle of incoming immigrants, of the "hordes" and the "swarms", that provokes this phantasy of gaps, in spite of there being leaders and governments still in power. Or perhaps there is a perception in these countries that their leaders are weak, ineffective, or corrupt, which then enables this sense of gaps.

The idea of the gap has, at its core, the people's fear around what will fill it. In addition, a re-finding of the gap, as in the hole in the flag, harks back, as in *après coup* or *Nachträglichkeit*, to unconscious memories and past fears, reaching back to the two world wars that were fought on European soil. Brexit is another large and heady addition to the formation of unconscious psychic gaps disrupting the old order, both the UK and Europe deeply disrupted in their forced separation. Yet another profound gap is looming with Trump's withdrawal of the US from the Paris climate agreement—threats that are made towards Mother Earth.

This does not mean that the gap, or Žižek's metaphor of the hole in the centre, cannot have value, however. If the gap is one of melancholic denial that wipes out thinking, it can lead to a manic, fractured national state of us vs them, and the continuation of aggressive state power. Yet the gap also holds the potential for an authentic state of mourning leading to creativity and aliveness in the individual as well as a template for establishing a better, fairer society.

The drive to repeat: the Polish Holocaust law

As noted earlier, the Polish president recently signed a bill, proposed by the Law and Justice party, criminalising any assertions of Polish participation in the Holocaust or other war crimes occurring under the German occupation of Poland. Comparisons were soon made between this law and the manipulations of historical narratives under Communism ("Poland's Holocaust Law Has Worrying Echoes", 2018). The newly ratified law states that anyone who "publicly and against the facts attributes to the Polish nation or state responsibility or co-responsibility for crimes perpetrated by the Third Reich will face prosecution", punishments ranging from a fine up to three years' imprisonment (ibid.). It does not make clear who will decide the historical "facts" that it references; neither does it clearly define the exempted categories of academics and artists (ibid.). The new legislation is very popular, and not just with Law and Justice supporters. The party's name seems strangely contradictory in light of this legislation, directed as it is against both of those concepts.

Marci Shore, a Yale historian, begins an article on the new law by quoting Freud in *Civilization and Its Discontents*: "Life, as we find it, is too hard for us … In order to bear it we cannot dispense with palliative measures" (Shore, 2018). Shore sees the Law and Justice party's current programme, which it labels "a good change" and also includes attempts to gain control of the media, and to introduce anti-abortion laws, as a series of such palliative measures (ibid.). This palliation clearly takes strange forms, these attempts to control the news and to control women's bodies depriving citizens of their freedom and leading society back towards totalitarian states of control.

In the case of the particular law regarding Polish involvement in the Holocaust and other war crimes, it has been explained as being a hugely disproportionate reaction to the oft-used shorthand "Polish death camps" when referring to the extermination camps operated in Poland by the Nazis ("Poland's Holocaust Law Has Worrying Echoes", 2018). At the European Psychoanalytic Congress in Warsaw in March 2018, the chilling effect of the new law was palpable, a sense of intimidation in advance about what is safe or unsafe to discuss under the gaze of this new law.

It is indisputable that in Poland during the Second World War there was active hostility towards Jews. One particularly notorious example is the massacre, on 10 July 1941, of between 200 and 400 Jews in the town of Jedwabne, near Białystock, part of Poland under Soviet occupation from 1939 to 1941. Jan Tomasz Gross's book about this massacre, *Neighbors*, first published in 2000, led to a crucial debate on the Holocaust in post-Communist Europe. The book pieces together, from eyewitness accounts, the massacre of Jedwabne's Jews by their Christian neighbours, who had known them through the entwining together of their lives. It was this book that, in 2006, under the first, short-lived Law and Justice government, provoked the initial attempts to outlaw accusations of Polish involvement in Nazi or Communist crimes. In response to the recent success of Law and Justice in passing this law, the Polish Centre for Holocaust Research responded: "We consider the adopted law a tool intended to facilitate the ideological manipulation and imposition of history policy of the Polish State" (Shore, 2018).

Another example of Polish hostility towards Jews that Gross's book made clear is the post-war pogrom that took place at Kielce in which 42 Jewish refugees, returning home from Auschwitz, were killed by Polish soldiers, police officers, and civilians (*The Kielce Pogram: A Blood Libel Massacre of Holocaust Survivors*). To escape such hatred and violence, many of the few thousand Polish survivors of the Holocaust decided to emigrate. In 2001, a year after the publication of *Neighbors*, President Aleksander Kwaśniewski laid a wreath at the site of the massacre, acknowledging that Poles were responsible and apologising on their behalf (Connolly, 2001).

It is worrying to note that the links we can recognise here between nationalism in Poland and the current government of the US are given extra weight by Trump's contact with Polish historian Marek Chodakiewicz. As Shore writes:

> Chodakiewicz, who has been among Mr Gross's most vicious attack-ers, and who now occupies a chair of Polish studies at the Institute of World Politics in Washington, wrote that the so-called March of Independence "grew from the need to demonstrate our pride in the fact that we belong to a historical continuity, which is worthy of defending against threats emerging from liberalism and lefty-ism, including Marxism-lesbianism and multiculturalism". The Polish press reported that President Trump consulted Mr. Chodakiewicz in preparing the speech [that Trump] delivered last July in Warsaw.
>
> (Shore, 2018)

Met here as we are by history beginning to repeat itself, it is perhaps apt to remind ourselves of Freud's descriptions in "Beyond the Pleasure Principle":

> There really does exist in the mind a compulsion to repeat which overrides the pleasure principle. Now too we shall be inclined to relate to this compulsion the dreams which occur in traumatic neu-roses and the impulse which leads children to play.
>
> (1920g, pp. 22–23)

How can we bring this understanding to bear on the vicious tropes we have been examining, buried in the minds of citizens to then return to the sur-face? In the current context, the underlying unconscious phantasies remain ready to become available to a national narrative at some particular his-torical juncture. Dreams bring to the surface unconscious wishes, and, as Freud writes, "May not dreams which, with a view to the psychical binding of traumatic impressions, obey the compulsion to repeat—may not such dreams occur *outside* analysis as well? And the reply can only be a decided affirmative" (ibid., p. 33). I suggest that this *"outside"*, this elsewhere, is the unconscious of socio-political life, in which a group wish can form to attack or kill a rival. In this way, individuals' desires to attack a sibling, or a parent, become diverted into hostile prejudices towards social others. These citizens, forming a throng that rallies around racist, anti-Semitic, and misogynistic tropes, thus feel free among the many who concur to actively support a group or political party that is overtly hostile towards the other.

Roger Money-Kyrle and the rhetoric of a Nazi rally

The psychoanalyst Roger Money-Kyrle was taken to a Nazi rally in 1932 at which both Hitler and Joseph Goebbels spoke. He writes with much interest on the experience of the large group dynamics:

> To primitive savages, calamities are never the result of impersonal forces. If they suffer from famine, disease or sudden death, they look for the sorcerer who, with his evil magic, has done these things. From our own more lofty standpoint we are apt to ridicule such primitive superstitions. But they tend to survive in our unconscious minds. The unconscious is aware of its internal enemies, and begins by attributing any new calamity to them. But if someone points to an external author, we are ready to believe him; for to fear and hate an external enemy at once lessens the internal tension. There is usually a small element of real truth, which is enormously exaggerated. Some people profited by the great slump, even if they did not create it. Some of these were Jews or Social-democrats. The orators had but to accuse them and to the audience in its semi-hypnotic trance, they were already proved guilty and convicted.
>
> (Money-Kyrle, 1941, p. 167)

Money-Kyrle compared the repetition in the orations, and its emotional effect, to that of Maurice Ravel's *Boléro*, hearing only three of four notes in the speeches. In both speeches, following the speaker's descriptions of Germany's sufferings since the First World War, the notes begin to grow louder, fulminating against the Jews and Social Democrats as being the sole causes of the country's troubles. Hitler concluded his speech with a plea for all Germans to unite, ending finally with, "Germany must live; even if we must die for her" (ibid. p. 166). As Money-Kyrle writes:

> No one asked who threatened Germany; and why the supreme sacrifice should be necessary. … At a single word from its leader, the monster was ready, indeed anxious, to immolate itself. (ibid.)

The rally crescendos from an "orgy of self-pity" (ibid.), the sufferings of poor Germany, through the blaming of two groups of others, to finally offering a manic cure for the terrors of helplessness:

> Self-pity and hatred were not enough. It was also necessary to drive out fear. … So the speakers turned from vituperation to self-praise. From small beginnings, the Party had grown invincible. Each listener felt a part of its omnipotence within himself. He was transported into a new psychosis. The induced melancholia passed into paranoia, and the paranoia into megalomania.
>
> (ibid., p. 168)

This excellent deconstruction of the art of propaganda deftly traces how a large audience can be swayed as one into a new belief in a self-righteous leader—one who promises that each member, by giving unswerving loyalty, will be able to take part in and benefit from a glorious resurgence of power. This megalomania, demanding the sacrifice of some groups, asserts that when the "enemy" is destroyed the group will ascend to fulfil its rightful destiny. It is unsettling to read David Livingstone Smith and Gwynn Guilford drawing out the similarities between Trump's style of rhetoric and that of the Nazi rally described by Money-Kyrle (Guilford, 2016). Hear the fear and hatred in this propaganda: only by destroying various groups—Muslims, immigrants from "shithole" countries, strong women—can America become great again.

The need for storytelling

Let me draw some of these diverse themes together around this chapter's opening thoughts on storytelling. When life moves, more or less, at an ordinary pace, the individual in a family, in a village, in a city can be part of a kind of connected fabric of life. Themes and variations in the news can be argued about and imagined. The fragments found in news items, Facebook, and gossip, while not deep narratives, can nonetheless constitute an imagination of the everyday, such that their storytelling has a containing function. However, in considerably more stressful times, where massive cruelties are being inflicted in different parts of the world and where neoliberal economics have led to huge increases in inequality, the idea of a hole in the centre, as Žižek's story of the flag reveals, may well be felt by individuals as a massive shock that can only be dealt with in primitive ways.

As Ferenczi found (see pp. 17–18), the individual reacts to massive trauma with splitting and atomisation, attempting to create a small mental space that is immune and safe from attack. The horrific stories we read earlier, concerning the plight of the Yazidi, convey those people's experiences in the centre of such a tear to the world they had been living in. They are shocking stories taking place in our world today and we do not know enough of the details. Vast numbers of the immigrants moving across the globe—from Afghanistan, Iraq, Syria, and other countries—each have their own harrowing stories; displacing themselves from torn, dangerous societies to cross borders, countries, and seas—hoping for safety and concern. They have a child's belief that, by moving away, someone will look after them. When they arrive, many people do want to provide that wished-for care. Yet the migrants' arrival is also preceded by an eruption of primitive phantasies in a proportion of the receiving population, fearful of being infected by the terrible experiences that the immigrants bring inside their minds. The result is a right-wing push to keep those "*Untermenschen*" away. Out of sight, out of mind: their stories must not be heard, because otherwise we will become like them.

I have been describing two similar metaphors: a gap and a tear, which can now, respectively, be regarded as an absence or an assault. The gap pertains to something gone, missing, perhaps lost, either temporarily or forever. For the abused child, the lost object might be the parent they loved and desired to be close to who then suddenly sexually attacks them. The loved object is lost, leaving a gap in the child's mind. The physical attack on the child's body follows this, penetration creating an actual tear in the body, such as the loss of the hymen, a physical assault that creates a psychic tear. This tear is more than the gap signifying the lost object. The tear created by paedophilia in the psychosomatic relationship is a sadomasochistic psychic development on the part of the adult attacker, and the child learns to accept and often to identify with this dynamic.

It can be argued that, in societies that are undergoing sudden and often unexpected change, such as in times of war or political insurgency, a gap that is similar to that resulting from child abuse appears in the usual running of the state. If the direction of the change is towards fundamentalism and strict control systems, this can also cause families to be torn apart. The stories told by the Yazidi confirm the sadistic tearings of family life and civilised governance that can lead to rape, torture, and murder. If it is felt that such stories must not be heard, then they must be replaced with narrow phantasies: that these refugees are lying, that they want to steal what we have, and that they have arrived to attack us. This is the model of identification with the aggressor, but in a double sense—the local inhabitants, fearing that the refugees somehow bring violence with them, defensively identify with that violence, directing it at the refugees. The local population also fears being ousted and themselves becoming refugees seeking safety elsewhere.

Again, the core of such structures is a severe tear in the centre of a society, with both immigrants and local inhabitants as potential victims. On the one hand, there is a fear that the immigrants will displace the locals, or that the locals are impacted in various ways by the influx; on the other hand, there is the potential for immigrants to be treated harshly and rejected. This structure also implies that the common rebalancing mechanism of seeking out a loving mother and father are expelled from thought.

The tear or split I am describing is that which can result from a receiving population's fear of being infected by the terrible experiences that immigrants might be bringing with them inside their minds, leading them to split off, shut out, and attack those immigrants in defence. Such splitting is the preferred, less imaginative option for so many, who thus hold on to their hate and aggression. Those who are more balanced in their lives, having had a good-enough, caring early life, may have enough resources to offer sustenance to the immigrant, without anxiety that more will be taken, leaving them depleted. Others, less fortunate, less cared for in their upbringing and in their present lives, will be paranoid that their plight is about to deteriorate even more. To take this metaphor further, when it is realised that the Yazidi are being cared for in Germany, and the tear in their society treated, a parallel tear appears unconsciously in parts of German society, followed by eruptions of hate, torment, and even killings of the damaged refugees. Nazism has appeared once more in large parts of former East Germany (and also in the West) and has found a new blame object.

In contrast to such fear-driven splitting, the attempt in Lublin to re-find lost stories, and the histories of murdered citizens, is an *après coup* demand for mourning and integration. It is similar to an analytic treatment, attempting to map lost terrains in the memories that are split off and repressed. Lanzmann tries something similar with *Shoah*, returning stories to life so that, both despite and because of the pain, through mourning, we can re-imagine that which has been defensively cast aside as unimaginable. It is painful to remember that Walter Benjamin, whose fiction was referenced above, despite having obtained a US visa from his friend Max Horkheimer, and despite being just a few miles from crossing the border into Spain, took an overdose of morphine. It seems, for him, that escape to freedom had become similarly unimaginable.

The recent assertions of Greek politician Yanis Varoufakis address with admirable clarity, in the context of Europe, the implications of the dynamics of splitting:

1. No European nation can be free as long as another's democracy is violated.
2. No European nation can live in dignity as long as another is denied it.
3. No European nation can hope for prosperity if another is pushed into permanent insolvency and depression.

(Varoufakis, 2016, p. 233)

In these terse statements, Varoufakis reminds us that freedom and dignity must be for all if democracy is to thrive. It is by acknowledging and knowing the traumatic states that can become embedded in the memories of groups, tribes, and nations, and by confronting the continual drip feeds of us vs them, insider vs outsider, complacent citizen vs fearful immigrant, that we can together partake, and thrive, in freedom.

I will end this chapter with one more story. The walled city of Harar in Ethiopia (the walls being built between the thirteenth and the sixteenth century) is full of very narrow alleyways. One street in the city, known as "The Street of Reconciliation", is particularly narrow—so much so that two people who have had a disagreement are unable to pass each other without communicating (Roberts, 2016). Having to walk through the narrowing of the passage, the two enemies are unable to avoid physical contact, and in this closeness lies the potential for reconciliation.

One can think of the problem that an individual brings to an analysis in the terms of this narrowing of a passage. The passing of time can bring rigidity to a person's thoughts and behaviour, with relationships harking back into early childhood remaining fundamentally unaltered in the adult. Yet the very persistence of these narrow relationships, fixed in the "old city" of the person's memory, gradually allows the possibility of rubbing up against their own fixity within the dyadic relationship with the analyst. New possibilities of relating can be imagined in this space and a daring project undertaken of loosening, branching out, and widening the sclerotic pathways. This is not to say that all of the person's relationships will blossom: some connections may refuse to budge due to the continued intransigence of the other. But there are still other, newer pathways that are able to move around. This might allow a person to develop away from the edge, from the border of their identity, and live their emotional life with a freedom that is far from the previous sense of immutability.

If such discoveries made in the consulting room can be profoundly transformative, perhaps these mental mechanisms can also be applied to individuals within groups, and even citizens within nations. Our task, as psychoanalysts, is to continue creating an environment in which there is the freedom to imagine the unimaginable, in all its formations, as a profound defence against the enactments of cruelty, both in families and in peoples. "Where do you still hear words from the dying that last, and that pass from one generation to the next like a precious ring?" is Benjamin's thoughtful plea (Benjamin, 1933, p. 731). Psychoanalysis has the potential, within its mental techniques, to open up and maintain such a space.

Endnotes

1. We can trace this brutal divide back to Napoleon's conquest of Egypt in 1798. Along with his troops, he also took scientists, engineers, and scholars tasked with documenting Egyptian culture, this resulting in a vast 23-volume encyclopaedia, *Description de l'Égypte* (published 1809–1828). Prior to this, in 1795, he had set up the Institute of France, and this enabled him to employ Enlightenment ideas as a form of colonisation. Ever since, Western ideologies have altered Islam in a profound way, provoking the transformation of the idea of Mohammed from a mystic into a rational Napoleonic figure—a lawgiver who organised society. A recent example of this is the revision of what has historically been the most widely spread narrative of Mohammed's marriage to Aisha,

which implies that she was six years old and that the marriage was consummated three years later. In light of the repugnance of the West today towards child marriage and paedophilia, the story of Mohammed's life, and hence Islam, has been refracted through so-called "enlightened" Western thinking. For some Muslims, however, this Western version of Islam is seen to be blasphemous, in Isis this leading to a need for a profound separation, cleansing their religion through the blood of apostates and demanding a return to its early pristine godhead and the firm divide between good and bad, for Islam or dead. The religious stories they hold sacred, thus, have the power to kill.

2. An example of a vision that counters splitting and hatred can be found in the thought that Norman Foster put into the rebuilding of the Reichstag, which has housed the German parliament since the reunification of Germany in 1990. As part of the restoration, a glass ceiling was installed beneath its dome so that visitors, standing above, can look down at the parliamentarians debating in the chamber below. It is an eloquent metaphor, the people above their politicians.

Cruelty in the early environment and its relationship with racism

In the Preface to the English edition of *If This is a Man*, Primo Levi wrote, "Many people—many nations—can find themselves holding, more or less wittingly, that every stranger is an enemy" (Levi, 1959, p. 9). Philippe Sands, writing ahead of a recent public reading of Levi's powerful memoir, asserted that:

> In the face of horror and oppression, Levi offers the possibility that humans will not easily—or completely—be demolished. … Have his books been read by a British prime minister who castigates those who feel a connection to the idea of global humanity as "citizens of nowhere"? Or read by a US president who wants to prevent human beings from entering his country simply because they are nationals of Somalia or Yemen or other countries deemed to be undesirable?
>
> (Sands, 2017)

And so we have been warned of the consequences of the fearful mentality that Levi describes, yet the liberal understanding is once again under great threat. It will remain so if people do not organise, from the grassroots up. This work should not be seen as tiresome: it should replenish emotional energy in the struggle against disempowerment.

Such disempowerment can often be a profound, unwelcome reminder of those childhood states of mind in which, for short or longer periods, we were pitched into silence and aloneness in the face of parental domination, whether perceived or actual. These unconscious reminders of the powerlessness of childhood can then provoke private phantasies of reversal. In adults who as children were under severe parental domination, the unconscious mind is available to reimagine the relationship, and may even desire, as talion (a law of "equivalent" retaliation, whereby the punishment resembles the offence committed), to kill the perceived object of control and belittlement. In a further leap of phantasy, the cruel parental imago can be retained and protected, and the feelings projected elsewhere, perhaps dumped onto objects of another race.

Such thoughts can be projected into a leader who allows and expects aggression to be directed, as in Trump's case, into racism and transphobia in order to inflame society, which he can then accuse of breakdown. He is thus enabled in invoking more controls and effecting a totalitarian rescue. It is the leader's aggression towards the other, now smeared as the architect of the subject's impoverishment, that demands revenge. A group is again blamed and we see projective mechanisms lead to increases in racism, Islamophobia, anti-Semitism, and misogyny. The previously hurt child who has never recovered from mental and physical childhood assaults joins the aggressive crowd and becomes loyal to his or her new family group. Not all emotionally lost children follow such an aggressive path, however. Perhaps those who do not are able to hold on to some kinder, more loving object, allowing a different character to emerge from the violent early chrysalis.

In this chapter, I want to examine how a cruel environment affects early development, leaving the child unable to believe in a secure, loving environment. I will also consider the impact of chronic social and political environments historically imbued with aggressive scapegoating of certain groups of citizens. Such racist, anti-Semitic, and misogynous cultures invariably work beneath the surface of society, attacking the ordinary fabric of family life in the provision of a particular model of perpetrators and victims—an unconscious playground in which to enact vicious games of us vs them. Children thus follow their parents' trajectory, identifying with their views. For many, siding with parental aggression against the other means they are less likely, in time, to become the victim themselves.

The origins of sadomasochism

In order to better understand some of the eruptions of hatred in society, I want to examine the theme of masochism central to Freud's paper "A Child Is Being Beaten" (1919e). Freud does not attempt to explain the origins of masochism, stating that "little light is thrown upon the genesis of masochism by our discussion of the beating phantasy". However, he describes the reconstructed phantasy of being beaten by father as "a convergence of the sense of guilt and sexual love", adding that "here for the first time we have the essence of masochism" (ibid., p. 189). What Freud is describing is the shifts in the phantasy as developments of unconscious constructions balance external reality at any given period of growing up. As Jack and Kerry Novick explain:

> The beating phantasy implies a particular type of relationship—one of power and submission. Freud delineates how it emerges out of the child's rage and humiliation at being dethroned from the position of sole recipient of parental love: from internal feelings of helplessness, hurt, and rage the child constructs the wish that the father should beat and so humiliate the despised rival. The transformation of the "sadistic" wish to the "masochistic" wish to be beaten by father is spurred by the internal changes of the oedipal phase, which lead the child into the wish to be the recipient of the father's love and to have his baby. Thus the 1919 paper contains a clear model for the object-relational component of sadomasochism.
>
> (Novick & Novick, 1997, pp. 37–38)

Freud's argument can be taken further by seeing that sadomasochism is a part of all object relationships, whether mild or pathological and perverse. We are all unconsciously both masochistic and sadistic with our objects and expect, in tandem or in talion, that our objects are with us. The point is rather the degree in which helplessness, hurt, and rage are refracted through a sadomasochistic relational screen, and so whether the impact on our character, and on how we relate to the other, is benign or malignant. This is affected by the impact of any childhood traumas on the child's unconscious phantasy life, which in turn depends on the vicissitudes both of family life through the generations and of the social milieu that the family inhabits and interacts with. The critical issue is whether such hurts continue to fester and resonate as desires for revenge, or whether, in a good-enough family environment, and with enough parental love, there is a coming to terms with the negative.

Freud notes that those who harbour beating phantasies develop a greater sensitivity and irritability towards father figures (Freud, 1919e). In a wider sweep, such "sensitivity" can lead to a pattern of identifying at times with the victim and at other times with the perpetrator, for some individuals a complex pluralism that oscillates between the two. Such sadomasochistic mechanisms can also be enacted against the self in psychosomatic forma-tions. Here, the conflict is taken beyond the unconscious mind and located on the body—the skin or the digestive system, perhaps, to name two of many possibilities. In these psychosomatic states, conflict becomes embod-ied (as itchiness/scratching, for example, or the bingeing/purging of buli-mia), defensively avoiding a felt emotion. Such psychosomatic formations occur when the mental impact is too much to process, such that the body is made available to bear the load, as it were, that the mind cannot.

Beating phantasies—that is, masochistic phantasies—are ubiquitous, always part of the formation of object relations, and an indispensable arena for the formation of character. It is the addition of actual childhood trau-mata that bites into character formation, adding the qualities of humilia-tion, despair, and angry revenge as potentialities, depending on whether the affect is projected or introjected. Whether the parents have the capacity to notice these impacts and assuage or elide severe cultural attacks on family life is a profound matter in the life of the child.

In "Letter to His Father", Franz Kafka writes an extraordinary example of the complexity of his thought processes in relation to the shadow of his father over his life:

> One night I kept on whimpering for water, certainly not because I was thirsty, but probably in order to be annoying and to amuse myself. After several vigorous threats had failed to have any effect, you took me out of bed, carried me out onto the *pavlatche* [balcony] and left me there alone outside the shut door for a while in my nightshirt. I am not saying that this was wrong (perhaps there was really no other way of getting any sleep that night), but I'm trying to characterize your methods of bringing up a child and their effect on me. I imag-ine I was quite obedient afterward, but it did me harm on the inside.

What was for me a matter of course, that senseless asking for water, and then the extraordinary terror of being carried outside were two things that I, my nature being what it was, could never properly connect. Even years afterward I suffered from the tormenting vision that the huge man, my father, the ultimate authority, would come almost for no reason and drag me out of bed in the night and carry me out onto the *pavlatche*, and that I meant absolutely nothing as far as he was concerned.

(Kafka, 1919, p. 65)

The easily humiliated Kafka was unable to use learning to escape a double bind: the more he studied, the more his father's autocratic command would elude his understanding. In the letter, Kafka is able to position himself outside of the conflict with his father, allowing him to describe rather than remain in its vortex. This becomes the fulcrum that allows him to describe paradoxical states of aggressors and victims that continue while making no sense, other than, this is the way in which life goes on. As he went through life, Kafka kept encountering this misanthropic paradox of obeying without understanding. His genius was to harness the whole set of paradoxical implications into the fabric of his creative writings. As Reiner Stach comments:

Josef K., the accused man in *The Trial*, is motivated by nebulous threats to focus all his energy on his trial and to comply with every one of the formalities, while being told that the law that underlies the procedure will remain unknowable even with a lifetime of effort. The surveyor K., the protagonist of *The Castle*, is ultimately undone by the same paradox; no matter how often he is told that he has no idea of how things actually work in the village, the explanations of the people he talks to keep revolving around mere procedural issues when K. tries to get to the bottom of things. It eventually becomes apparent that the villagers themselves are mystified by their world.

(Stach, 2017, p. 131)

And so Kafka transformed the humiliations of his childhood into a creative life that describes the paradox and gives it transcendence. As well as describing being captive to either the victim or the aggressor, with no escape, he allows the reader to see with more and more clarity the perpetual nature of the system—that the system is not just corrupt but fixed and self-perpetuating, unless an act of freedom occurs.

In *The Castle*, we can also catch a glimpse of the villagers' mystification regarding life, as if the people cannot really know what they are doing in their identification with the cruel phenomena in their culture. Their preference for mystification is striking and strange when we consider their position of confusion and unknowing alongside their eagerness for law, etiquette, and custom. It is easy to sense that this blind adherence to false rules—being overly compliant and believing intensely in custom—is another example of identification with the aggressor, becoming the handcuffs that prevent a freedom of thought, a fixity against necessary action.

Kafka's dramatising of these mystifications allows the possibility of thinking past them, though, and so of mobilising against their constraints. These narratives of breaking free are a common literary device of children's comics familiar as "with one bound he was free"; the protagonist is always able to escape, no matter how dangerous and complex the cliffhanging has become.

Masochism re-examined

Freud wrote "A Child Is Being Beaten" following the First World War, the end of which, rather than bringing only relief, also brought continuing difficulties in finding work and food. He had difficulty feeding his family until about 1920. Through long exposure to war and its emotional and physical derivatives, Freud became attuned to the question of psychic violence, and was thus led to describe the death and destructive drive.[1] His 1919 paper can thus be situated in a wider societal context of the abuses of power and the sense and impact of being beaten and of suffering. Later, he gave consideration to political and social systems, such as those in which he aimed to more deeply understand identification with the father-leader who beats by projective mechanisms while looking after his people (for example, Freud, 1921c).

Freud's analysis of masochism is clearly a source of great insight, but it has a significant blind spot. Where is the mother in the paper that continuously returns in every developmental position to the father? As has been pointed out by the Novicks, this is Freud's "glaring omission": "Freud does not mention the mother at all in relation to his female patients and refers to the oedipal mother only with the males" (Novick & Novick, 1997, p. 40). Even in the oral phase, it is the masochistic fear of being eaten by Father that is described, wiping out the mother's primary and feeding role in reality and in the early constructions of the part-object relational beginnings of "me" and "not me" as the object relationship between self and mother emerge.

This omittance of the primary importance of the maternal register leads to an equation of femininity, passivity, and the masochistic position. As Donald Winnicott describes, the theory of there being a natural masochism in women is a false one (Winnicott, 1947, p. 202). Therefore, if the mother is also, in addition to the father, at times a power-refracting object, all the arguments about the supreme importance of the paternal object to the development of sadomasochistic phantasies at once fall, shifting the developmental terrain into even more complex webs of two- and three-person psychology. This becomes the area of Melanie Klein in the shift from paternal to maternal and, in particular, the infant's relation to the maternal body. Yet Freud did not recast the social theories of the primal horde and the murder of the father in the light of his discovery of pre-oedipality and the importance of Mother.

Winnicott explains the falsity of the theory of a natural female masochism as follows:

> A mother has to be able to tolerate hating her baby without doing anything about it. She cannot express it to him. If, for fear of what she may do, she cannot hate appropriately when hurt by her child she must fall back on masochism, and I think it is this that gives rise to the false theory of a natural masochism in women. The most remarkable thing about a mother is her ability to be hurt so much by her baby and to hate so much without paying the child out, and her ability to wait for rewards that may or may not come at a later date. Perhaps she is helped by some of the nursery rhymes she sings, which her baby enjoys but fortunately does not understand?
>
> > 'Rockabye Baby, on the tree top,
> > When the wind blows the cradle will rock,
> > When the bough breaks the cradle will fall,
> > Down will come baby, cradle and all.'
>
> (ibid.)

The baby's hatred needs to meet its match in either the mother or the father, not enacted with blows or perversity but as an unconscious counterbalancing matrix that contains that hatred from the baby. In this situation, the rhyme that Winnicott quotes is not sentimental and is probably sung with an unconsciousness about what it describes. Yet as a response to the upturning of the mother's life, subsequent to the birth of her baby, it gives the mother a chance to imagine the baby falling out of its cradle, the mother's arms. In the mother's unconscious phantasy, her freeing herself from the baby, and the baby crashing to the ground, for a moment allows her an internal mental space that contains her hatred of the baby and baby's impossible demands, freeing her of the need to actually retaliate. This is an act of freedom. However if this contains too much of an opposite direction of internal guilt it can lead the mother into a lifetime direction of masochism towards other objects. This is subject to the mother's own unconscious knowledge of how her own mother dealt with her baby's demands years before, balancing her "good enough" capacities and the intensity of her baby's needs and character.

Hatred of the other

Thus far, I have directed attention to the propensity of the damaged child to project him or herself, as an adult, into joining the sadism of a leader who encourages hatred against a particular "other-ed" group. I suggest that this is due to the heightened level of excitation available, as well as the offered possibility of belonging. The double dilemma of feeling dull, perplexed, bored, and stuck together with feeling alone gives way to an eruption of hope in joining a group that offers involvement in a wave of violence, and so the opportunity to feel alive. The child who was beaten now inflicts the beating elsewhere. This is a quick fix such that the beaten-child–grown-up can regress into states of excitement and empowerment, far removed from having to remain in his or her own solitary victimhood. However, if one follows the other pathway, it means that the masochism of staying the victim, as an adult, prevails. This possibility can be seen in the enormous increase in severe addictive states due to heroin, cocaine, and chronic marijuana consumption. In this position, the addict identifies with the aggressor in the belief that he or she is in control of achieving the "fix"—which is in fact an attack on the self. Rather than projecting the aggression onto an outside object, it is now directed against the self.

To take the US as the exemplar, Trumpism has deliberately exposed a deep, chronic hatred—one that has again become conscious, expressed openly by the Ku Klux Klan (KKK) and neo-Nazis, as well as the new "alt-right". The massive outbreak of active attacks on certain groups has been encouraged both by Trump's statements and the discriminatory policies he has been trying to pass into law. Such widened schisms in society then further enable the president to take fascistic control. A huge deterioration in the hopes of young people, white and black, also accompanies this, however, and, as their attitude towards their society becomes one of resignation, they often turn passively inwards to the solipsism of a life numbed with drugs. We can thus trace both active and passive attacks as the two arcs of possibility resulting from the detritus of a childhood tainted by hate, perhaps due to the unconscious hatred directed towards an unwanted child coming into the family, inflicted by mothers, fathers, and others.

The reader will have detected the absence of potential states of healing in these descriptions. In response to this, I refer to Winnicott's concept of the "good enough mother" in its embrace of the idea that no childhood is perfect. The many ups and downs of any childhood include profound moments when the care given was just plain wrong. For instance, the young child who is unable to communicate to the parent what she or he wants is left frustrated, angry, and despairing, while the parent, unable to fathom what is damaging their child's well-being, starts to feel the same. In addition to this, how parents either welcome or do not welcome a next child into family life is the matrix through which the child born earlier tries to understand what is happening. The later pregnancy might have been desired or it might be hated. A failed abortion can silently echo as the alert older child picks up on its ghostly presence.

But the state of a "good enough" upbringing can form an endowment in which much is understood and done well. In time, this can allow the realisation that the world is not all bad, along with the developing understanding in the child that bad states can and will be recovered from. This is not the case for children who have lived too much in the shadow of assaults of many kinds, leading to an overall state of despair and an inability to believe in love, humanity, respect, and the possibility of restitution. This can lead to a sense of generational trauma in which historical oppression and its negative consequences are passed on. When such children grow up they usually stay in the shadows of life and love, managing more or less, but with deeply impoverished object relationships. It is this large group that, encouraged by impassioned dictatorial leaders, can erupt into hatred of the other.

Let us now examine the situation from the opposite direction—the unconscious influence of the social and political environment on family life and the subsequent impact of this on the developing mind of the child. The recent film *I Am Not Your Negro*, a documentary about the writer and social critic James Baldwin, shows footage of howling young white males, some only boys, carrying placards with swastikas as they bear down on black children escorted to school by the National Guard (Peck, 2016). They pass through a gauntlet of raging white faces in Little Rock, Arkansas. It goes on to document Baldwin's debate with William Buckley Jr at the Cambridge University Union in 1965, on the motion "Is the American Dream at the Expense of the American Negro?" Baldwin ended his speech with the statement: "What has happened to white southerners is much worse than what has happened to negroes there." Baldwin's radical thought describes how the outbreak of social venom picks the wrong modern object because there has been no mental integration of earlier childhood states of rage and despair, leading later to an outbreak of revenge on a whole other group. There is no reckoning of the past, let alone mourning, while riding high on an identification with the aggressor. Instead, a victim is found, either new or old—in this case, utilising racism—to allow the now grown-up hurt child to feel empowered, identifying with the aggression that was once directed at themselves. As the traumatised child grows up, unhealed and without mourning, society can direct the unconscious shame, hatred, and isolation that they once felt—from having been the child victim of an aggressive adult, perhaps—into an identification with the aggressor. The new rationale is: "I am no longer the victim: they are. I can scream at them and humiliate them and, as was the case for me, no one will stop it, and no one will speak out against it." This pathological method of recovering from childhood states of humiliation is thus to join a group that attacks and humiliates others.

To my mind, this is a leading formation of societal attacks against a variety of objects. Racism, Islamophobia, anti-liberality, misogyny, and the old tropes against Jews are all available to enable the satisfying position of attacking and humiliating the other. In each, the other is the hated object and the subject is hidden within the sadism of the new order. As the attacked child knows (as Kafka makes clear in his powerful letter), the sadistic adult is all powerful and gets away with all of their crimes against them.

Racist violence in the US

To explore in more detail the diverse forms in which violence against the other often still pervades society, we can consider the racism that runs through and defines the US and its institutions. Bryan Stevenson reminds us of the history of this violence with great clarity:

> People of color in the US, particularly young black men, are often assumed to be guilty and dangerous. ... As a consequence of this country's failure to address effectively its legacy of racial inequality, this presumption of guilt and the history that created it have significantly shaped every institution in American society, especially the criminal justice system. ... Between the Civil War and World War II, thousands of African-Americans were lynched in the United States. ... These racially motivated acts, meant to bypass legal institutions in order to intimidate entire populations, became a form of terrorism. ... [In the twelve former slave states, Alabama, Arkansas, Florida, Georgia, Kentucky, Louisiana, Mississippi, North Carolina, South Carolina, Tennessee, Texas, and Virginia, there were over] four thousand racial terror lynchings between 1877 and 1950. ... Of the hundreds of black people lynched after being accused of rape and murder, very few were legally convicted of a crime. ... Hundreds more black people were lynched based on accusations of far less serious crimes, like arson, robbery, nonsexual assault, and vagrancy, many of which would not have been punishable by death even if the defendants had been convicted in a court of law. In addition, African-Americans were frequently lynched for not conforming to social customs or racial expectations, such as speaking to white people with less respect or formality than observers believed due. ... Some "public spectacle lynchings" were even attended by the entire local white population and conducted as celebratory acts of racial control and domination. ... [Such] lynching and racial terror motivated the forced migration of millions of black Americans out of the South. ... The northern states had abolished public executions by 1850, [but] some in the South maintained the practice until 1938. ... Following Will Mack's execution by public hanging in Brandon, Mississippi, in 1909, the *Brandon News* reasoned: "Public hangings are wrong, but under the circumstances, the quiet acquiescence of the people to submit to a legal trial, and their good behavior throughout, left no alternative to the board of supervisors but to grant the almost universal demand for a public execution."
>
> (Stevenson, 2017)

Of course, this is a well-known method used by the establishment, pleasing the people with a scene of violence and cruelty inflicted on the other, while simultaneously establishing fear in the community. The killing of slaves in the Roman Colosseum, the public burnings at the stake of the Spanish Inquisition, the public beheadings by Oliver Cromwell, and the use of the guillotine during the French Revolution were all within the ambit of entertainments for the population, but racial violence in the US has outlasted all such reigns of terror. Stevenson notes that "the Civil Rights Act of 1964, arguably the signal legal achievement of the Civil Rights Movement, contained provisions designed to eliminate discrimination in voting, education, and employment, but did not address racial bias in criminal justice" (ibid.). Unsurprisingly, it is within this lacuna that massive systematic racism has been preserved, outlawed Confederate lynching being replaced by the imprisonment of black citizens in their millions, and with an absence of federal protection against racial bias in the use of the death penalty. As Stevenson summarises, "the modern American death penalty has its origins in racial terror" (ibid.).

Within the first year of the Trump administration—with Trump's support of the Confederacy-based KKK and the overt Nazism of the alt-right—thousands of Americans have begun to stand up against the old–new terror tactics. Yet let us examine this area more deeply. Despite the Confederates losing the Civil War, there has been a continual nurturing of the racial history of those states. Cities and towns are adorned with statues celebrating racist "heroes". A dark strand of American life, expressed partly in its addiction to gun culture, subsists and has developed, waiting for unconscious hatred to emerge. The weapon harks back in time to the slave owners and the white population being those with arms. The slaves were unarmed and vulnerable to the gun-holding white other. Is this any different for black people than for the shtetl Jews living under the similarly violent shadow of the next pogrom? And what then is the impact of this on family life, both for the victims and those families of the supposed master race?

Ghettoisation and the black child meeting the white world

Another way of framing this question is to consider the psychological impact of ghettoisation, both on those who live in the ghetto and those who do not. Ghetto children grow up noticing but not understanding the presumption of guilt that they live under, despite being terrified from time to time by the violent eruptions where they live. This mystification can lead to the development of many different neurotic debilities, often based on a sense that the child's parents are not strong enough to create a safe family environment that the child can identify with and internalise. When outside of the relative safety of home, these children learn to read the streets and their potential dangers, but they are ultimately left with the non-understanding that it is their skin colour that turns them, whatever they might do, into potential victims. Skin colour ought to be an ordinary variable, like hair colour or height, but this is not the case with blackness vs whiteness. Knowing that one is the victim is simple enough to know but it is less understandable with regard to why skin colour is the pointer of the racist's prejudice.

Frantz Fanon's statement is interesting in this context, that "a normal black child, having grown up with a normal family, will become abnormal at the slightest contact with the white world" (Fanon, 1952, p. 122). In a way, this scenario is ubiquitous; all children growing up in a family of one sort or another will find that, when they venture outside out of the family, meeting other children at school, their view that all children are treated like them is challenged. It is common for children who grow up in families in which they feel unloved, or even hated, to imagine finding a "good" mother at a friend's house, enabling them for a moment to sink into the pleasure of the idea of being lovingly held, with a nourishing tea or a warm, uncritical atmosphere; yet the return to their own emotionally empty home dashes the reverie.

Depending on the emotional atmosphere at home, if the black child's meeting of the white world is hurtful, it can be held and understood in a "good enough" home environment. The same is true of the white child. The knocks that a child receives from having to face the reality of the real world can be mitigated, soothed, and understood when they return home. Sometimes, such a thoughtful home environment is not available, however, leading to different developmental paths that can progress into the reality of growing up in a family environment that accepts prejudice.

Let us turn now to James Baldwin's concern for the damage this violence can also wreak on the racist white family. Children in such families can grow up in an environment of superiority, believing that those others are beneath them in intelligence, apparently because they do not have white skin. They can potentially develop an identification with the aggressor as a normative activity, so that the possibility of projecting blame onto another group becomes ordinary; they thus develop the idea of a high-minded "us" and a lowly "them". After testing this out in the classroom, the family confirms that violence against blacks or Jews is acceptable; their child's attacks thus are supported.

Baldwin's statement, that "what has happened to white southerners is much worse than what has happened to negroes there" (see p. 62), might perhaps seem very unusual, implying as it does that being the attacker in this instance is worse than being the victim. Perhaps his understanding is that white racists have more work to do than their black victims if they seek to disengage themselves from their unconscious sense of superiority. This racist psychology of superiority has a social stickiness to it that can be difficult to get free of, especially as this task might demand that the white would-be-ex-racist create a distance from his or her own racist family. The family might then turn on the deserter and "colour them black", turning that individual too into a victim of the family's racism.

Horizontalism: deceits and manipulations

It is easy to recognise that the normalised, everyday racism, learnt by white children from their families, is one with the more formalised racism that can be found in all sections of wider society. In addition to the racism of the criminal justice system that we noted above, we can add the pseudoscience historically developed on the subject, trying to define the characteristics of black people. The nineteenth century, for example, saw the invention of disorders such as "dysaesthesia aethiopica" (rascality in blacks free and enslaved) and "drapetomania" (a tendency among the enslaved to flee captivity) (Morrison, 2017, p. 58). Such perversion of science is similarly found in Nazi propaganda about Jewish facial stereotypes. Today, rather than being rejected completely, evolutionary theory is subsumed into creationism, so that it can continue to be taught in schools, and so that narrow Christian fundamentalism is allowed to flourish.

Clearly, then, the idea written by Thomas Jefferson in the US Declaration of Independence, that "all men are created equal", is only a beautiful idealisation rather than a reality. The child finds it to be a perverse corruption of the truth of society, both inside and outside the family home. Parents are not equal to their children, and often a pecking order exists between siblings, older children occupying a higher position in many ways than later children. In addition, a rivalry can exist between siblings in ascertaining who might be loved most by their parents. This conscious and unconscious search for one's place in the hearts and minds of one's parents is a matrix out of which the character of object relationships develops. When such pecking orders are tested against reality, often a child who is unwanted does not find themselves to be very highly desired by their family: "Why do I always get a lesser portion than him/her?" Or if the special one has, in fact, to be one of the parents, the child might find that a life of appeasement is preferable to upsetting the narcissism of that parent, and so will avoid confronting them, leaving the hierarchy to continue festering. This can occur in any family, black or white.

In "Psychoanalysis in the Age of Bewilderment: The Return of the Oppressed", Christopher Bollas defines a new concept, "horizontalism", as that which does not recognise hierarchical order:

> All things are equal and no one thing is intrinsically more important than another. ... The recognized value of the opinions of highly experienced journalists, scholars, and writers now fades out as the social democracy of the internet turns everyone into an expert on any topic. While this democratization is hugely beneficial in many respects, the down side is the inadvertent promotion of the power of the uninformed self.
>
> When vertical thinking is destroyed and horizontal thought prevails then *difference* between one topic or another becomes meaningless. Indeed, differentiation is predicated on the ability to evaluate and to discriminate between objects; to find in alterity a tensional creativity as difference generates oppositions that will be valued if heterogeneity is assumed to be of value. But the process of globalisation promotes a global-self, a uniform being that even if only ever a fiction (it could never become a reality) may nonetheless function as a psychic soporific for homogenized human beings. So, to operationalism and horizontalism we add homogenization: the need to eradicate difference and fashion a world of common beings. The promotion of homogeneity aims at the reduction of difference, the lessening of tensions, and the presumed increase in the productive potential of the human being.
>
> (Bollas, 2015, p. 544)

We can see a clear examples of such horizontalism in Trump's support of the KKK and neo-Nazis that marched into Charlottesville[2]—with tiki torches,

Confederate flags, Nazi slogans, swastikas, and banners reading "Jews will not replace us"—when he openly equated the behaviour of the antifascists who protested the march with that of the fascists, saying there were "pretty bad dudes" on both sides. Trump's horizontalism presents two opposing positions—anti-racists are the same as racists—such that we have no need to think and discriminate between different orders of things.

In our narrowing world, reduced to the limits of a Twitter post and a Facebook like, all is moving towards sameness. And in the absence of us, the people, exercising our capacities to think, we become suckers for a take-over by the totalitarian father who really 'knows' and who will lead us into a violent and hating world. Trump and other such leaders milk this abject, angry support to move further towards controlling, totalitarian goals. Unbeknownst to their supporters, the leader has no concern for them and will not hesitate to sacrifice the mob, repeating the past failings of uncaring parents to provide a sufficient holding of the child. These leaders' horizon-talist rhetoric is one of deceit, manipulating followers with racism and other tropes that target the other.

Revealing racism in South Africa

Some years ago, in one of an annual series of psychoanalytic conferences in South Africa that Professor Mark Solms—South African psychoanalyst and neuropsychologist—and I developed, we decided on the all-too-obvious theme of racism. The conference was focused mainly on confronting, con-taining, and thinking about the incipient racism in the cases that were being treated, in the context of the pervasive socio-political atmosphere of his-toric racism that continues to stain every part of South African society.

At the start of the conference of around 80 participants, a white partici-pant asked one of the few black participants, "Why are there so few of you?" The instant reply was, "Why do you think it is for us to answer rather than you?" This interchange, with its perceptively sublime response, hovered darkly, unanswered, over the proceedings. Sometime later, a black nurse began to laugh, unable to stifle her mirth. She was encouraged to speak and eventually told a story. She had been trained and then worked in a local black hospital. One day, however, there was a sudden outbreak of some infection at the Groote Schuur Hospital, and, after many of the white nurses became sick and had to take time off, a contingent of black nurses was drafted in to help. After being allocated to a ward, the nurse had to deliver a bedpan to an old white female patient. The patient then rang to inform her that the task was finished and so the nurse took the pan to the sluice. She now peeled with laughter, bemusing the rest of us. Eventually, she collected her words and told us of the astonishment she had felt at seeing that the white patient's shit was not also white, and that it was, in fact, black. This had conflicted with her phantasy system, in which she had assumed that white people had white shit while black people had black shit. She was laughing incredulously at the collapse of her belief system. By now, we were all laughing and the group was emotionally one, rather than one member being affectively out of kilter. Yet, the nurse's story had allowed the point to be made that both blacks and whites had developed unconscious phantasies of the other in an attempt to "make sense" of the massive racist culture, both known but also deeply unconscious, that had held sway for well over a century.

To put the matter more bluntly, the material from the conference on racism allowed an understanding in the room that we are all racist in our unconscious minds. The nurse's critique of the apparent liberality of the white organisers freed us to notice that we were all guilty of harbour-ing thoughts of us and them. These admissions could then be shared and discussed, leading to a concomitant relieving of guilt and a coming closer together of all participants, whatever the colour of their skin. The dark cloud within each of us, whichever corner we were standing in, had been revealed. Within the conference, the whites were not in a state of power over the blacks, or vice versa. The position we were able to reach, and its subse-quent exploration, was the opposite of the deceitfulness of horizontalism, which in its superficiality leads us all towards having the same thoughts. It required a great deal of grappling with the unconscious phantasies that the different cultures, from black and white upbringings, maintained as forms of protection against the other. At the end of the conference, we left with a profound, deepened sense of ownership of our own unconscious racism, without the need to project it immediately elsewhere.

I do not think that the participants of the annual conference could have reached such a mature position without several years of working together annually, alongside daily analytic thinking, in which they had immersed themselves. This work allowed a deep-enough sense of trust in the confer-ence as able to contain contradictory unconscious phantasies about what the other thought—that the white majority preferred there to be few blacks in attendance, for example, as a perverse way of staying on top of the racist pecking order. The use of free association was key in this process of opening up, the uncontrollable laughter from one colleague leading her to share a story that perfectly enabled the attendants of the conference to face their internal prejudices. How even more impressive it would be if larger groups in society could similarly openly face such dark thoughts.

Monuments and mourning

In the first chapter, I wrote of several monuments that have been erected in order to remember, and I considered some that I see as being erected for other purposes—the monument in Berlin on the site of the Nazi's burning of the books, for example. While the concrete library is evocative, spiralling below the ground, from just a few paces away, it is invisible to passers-by; this results in an ambivalence, as if it does not really need to be seen. Other monuments, however, succeed in inviting the viewer in the present to be in touch with the past, and in directing unconscious attention to aspects of mourning. A clear example of the latter would be the room full of thousands of pairs of old shoes, in every size, that had been owned and worn by Jews killed in Auschwitz, along with huge mountains of old leather cases that had once held their last possessions before their departure to a camp, and, most likely, to their death. The sight is unequivocal and real, each item long-ago owned and used by an individual who became one of many thousands imprisoned and murdered for their race.

Standing in the presence of these objects, clearly from the past, is a profound signifier of all that has been lost. This wave of history meeting the onlooker's senses enables a "being in the experience" at that moment (and usually, in its aftermath, for much longer) that profoundly resonates with death and with the way these people died. Seeing all this stirs thoughts, associations, memories, and gaps in one's mind, and there is an intense pain in this confronting of what really did happen. Continuing such an internal journey might lead to the development of ideas, such as "Never again" or "What would I have done if that had happened to me, or my parents, or my children?" A personification of the sense of loss invades and upsets the usual defences used to maintain a distance from such terrible matters— the simplest of which is the disbelief that such events actually happened. Indeed, there is much support in the community—and, from time to time, in the politics of a country—in turning away from such sad, strange thoughts, even to sink into the stories that the neo-Nazis tell, which say that these histories are false. In these stories, the victims are turned into the perpetrators of these supposed historical lies and claimed as evidence of continuing Jewish world domination. They were not really murdered in their millions; rather, the world has readily swallowed a lie spread by those purported victims, who actually have control over you and your life.

Our susceptibility to disbelieving in human cruelty—indeed, in the apparent "inhumanity" of humans—is huge. Tyrannical leaders swiftly move to facilitate this disbelief by dismantling the press as soon as they take power, thus guiding the population away from the nightmares of the sadistic realities of the past that might be recalled by the methods of the new regime. This is one of the key battles in the US currently, Trump affirming that most journalists are liars peddling fake news, encouraging the people to slumber on while their freedom to think and to be is taken away.

And so to the pulling down of Confederate monuments in the US—one of the key battles against the racist mind being fought under Trumpism. Confederate monuments and memorials were built for leaders or soldiers or to honour the Confederate States of America. There are some 1,500 such symbols of the Confederacy in public spaces in the US, placed overwhelmingly in the states of the old Confederacy. In her Introduction to *Monuments to the Lost Cause*, Cynthia Mills states that the majority of Confederate monuments were commissioned by white women "in the hope of preserving a positive vision of antebellum life" (Mills, 2003, p. xvi). These women were members of groups such as the United Daughters of the Confederacy or the Ladies' Memorial Associations. How strange that many such commemorations of Confederacy dead, and of the loss of slavery—which was the battle that the Southern states lost against the North—were paid for by Southern belles. In Grant Woods' satirical painting, *Daughters of Revolution*, we have conveyed to us the stern superiority of this class of white Southern women. The three subjects gaze at us confidently, one with a wry smile and another's mannered holding of her china teacup reveals a chillingly smug sense of self-righteousness. They evoke the powerful idea that there is nothing really wrong that a quiet cup of tea cannot resolve, and so the sanctimonious sense that really there is no problem in an America beset by race wars. This abundance of monuments erected by such women of the Confederacy suggests unconscious associations with the idea of white women long being at the mercy of black men, who are now unbridled. The idea that black men want to rape and kill white women is one of the disturbing, unconscious racist tropes that are still active. This unconscious belief becomes a twisted reason for the continuation of American racism and the imprisonment or murder,

Daughters of Revolution, Grant Wood, 1932, oil on masonite.

by police and others, of so many black men. Perhaps all of this is still to protect the Southern belle.

Most Confederate monuments were not erected immediately following the end of the Civil War in 1865. Commemorative markers made at that time tended to mourn soldiers who had died. The vast majority were built between the 1890s and the 1950s—the era of Jim Crow segregation—and they were built to glorify the Civil War and its cause. The South was also romanticised in general, a prime example being *Gone with the Wind*, and as a consequence, slavery too was romanticised, even in *Uncle Tom's Cabin*, despite its status as an anti-slavery novel. Similar later constructions can be seen as a "backlash" to the Civil Rights Movement (this word appropriately echoing the "lashing" that the Confederate descendants might have wished to inflict once again). In 1956, for example, Georgia redesigned its state flag to include the Confederate battle flag. In 1962, South Carolina placed the flag atop its capitol building. This return of the repressed is a reminder that American racism is still alive and well in the Southern states and that the argument for slavery—the central element of the war between the Northern and Southern states—continues, now just beneath the surface in an unreconstructed manner. These monuments, far from just commemorating the war dead from a particular battle, now occupy space that reminds, goads, and lashes the onlooker with the open assertion that the division between slave owners and slave victims is still desired by many white Americans. They also keep alive unconscious hopes that the Confederacy's loss of the war will one day be reversed.

After nine black churchgoers were killed in a racially motivated massacre in Charleston, South Carolina, in 2015, the city council in New Orleans ordered the removal of several monuments honouring the Confederacy. This started a larger, nationwide movement to remove other symbols of the rebellion, including Confederate flags. The activism of the Black Lives Matter movement is essential and accurate precisely because of this partly silent, tenacious phantasy world performed and inhabited by white supremacists. Trump stokes this agenda, telling us all that there "is blame on both sides" following the neo-Nazi rally in Charlottesville and framing opposition to the racists as part of the problem. There are "very fine people" among those in the rally, he says, as white supremacists and neo-Nazis spit out hatred of blacks and Jews, aligning themselves with Hitlerian slogans such as "blood and soil".

It is hard to believe that there have been no memorials yet built in the US for the victims of lynching. Yet the sites of these lynchings—spectacles affirming white power through terrorism of black communities—are invariably well known, often outside Southern courthouses still in use today. Even some of the trees that once bore "strange fruit" are still standing. However, this total wiping out and ignoring of so many racist murders is about to change with the Equal Justice Initiative's construction of a museum in Montgomery, Alabama, which will commemorate victims of lynching across the South. The names of around 4,000 black victims of lynching between 1877 and 1950 will be engraved on a series of columns, each representing a county in which the lynching took place. I believe that this museum is only the start of what might become a new programme of openness and honesty about the murders that were perpetrated in the US.

In Berlin today, the names of Jewish shop owners who were removed and taken to their deaths in concentration camps are engraved at the entrance of many shops. This is history brought into the present to impact on a personal level as one walks over the threshold. The confronting of the truth of a state-organised mass-murder, despite its inevitable pain, is liberating to the humanity in each of us. A similar national project could sweep over the US, so that local memorials stating who was hanged, when, and by whom would become a central, visible part of American towns and cities for both residents and visitors. This could be an important contribution to the fight against the present wave of false news designed to obscure truth, and it might help to make possible, in time, a new sense of reconciliation. It could act as container for the mother who can know, see, and honour the place of her murdered child. Reconciliation over those many deaths would be a memorial, showing that black lives matter, the continuum of the beatings of racism thus being reduced. The ghosts of the victims of racism will now have a role in the places where lynching took place: in the towns, outside the old courthouses, and from certain trees still standing. The thoughts and behaviour of the perpetrators thus no longer allowed, either physically or imaginatively, to dominate the terrain.

Endnotes

1. For those interested in learning more about the death and destructive drive, it is extensively reviewed in *Balint Matters* (Sklar, 2017, pp. 8–11).

2. On 11 to 12 August 2017, a rally was held in Charlottesville, Virginia, United States, to oppose the removal of a statue of Robert E. Lee from Charlottesville's Emancipation Park. It was attended by a number of far-right and white supremacist groups and the event turned violent after clashes with counter-protesters, leaving many injured on both sides. Alongside this, a car rammed into a group of people peacefully protesting, killing one person and injuring nineteen. In a separate incident, two police officers died when their helicopter, which was monitoring the far-right rally, crashed. The event became known as the "Charlottesville riots" (Wilson et al., 2017).

Epilogue

No one can truly know himself
Detach himself from his innermost being
Yet still he must test, each day
What he clearly sees from without
What he is, what he was
What he can do, and what he stands for

—Goethe: "Zahme Xenien"

As I was just finishing this manuscript, I heard a performance of Richard Strauss' *Metamorphosen* under the baton of Pappano at Covent Garden. In the programme notes, I read that on 2 October 1943, an Allied bombing raid destroyed the Munich National Theatre. Strauss, born there, described the desecration as "the greatest catastrophe which has ever been brought into my life, for which there can be no consolation" (Bratby, 2018).

Worse, on 2 March 1945, after hearing of the firebombing of Dresden, he wrote, "I am in despair! The Goethaus, the world's greatest sanctuary destroyed! My beautiful Dresden, Weimar, Munich—all gone" (ibid.). Ten days later, the Vienna State Opera burned to the ground. This fired him to write *Metamorphosen* as a great lament for the destruction of a civilisation.

As Richard Bratby writes:

A final, impassioned climax totters into an equally final collapse, and the music of the opening returns, destined this time to lead only downwards into C-minor darkness where the source of the transformation becomes clear: and a fragment of the funeral march from Beethoven's *Eroica* symphony stands blackened in the basses. Strauss wrote the words 'IN MEMORIAM' over its broken remains.

(ibid.)

Strauss was offering the world a requiem of the devastation of war destruction against centuries-old culture created by the people. He knew that beyond the burning buildings was the Nazi persecution of the Jews, including his daughter-in-law and family. The music is themed with darkness, and despite an uplift, it returns to a deeply sombre and searing ending. It is too much to mourn the enormity of what has happened. And the lines from Goethe are for all of us, as yet untested, unknowing of how we will manage to realise that we will each decide: "What he can do and what he stands for."

During the last five years, since 2014, the West has been in the grip of a century's return to the start of the Great War. Narratives, books, films, and memorial events have put us back in those increasingly terrible times that led to the deaths of many millions—soldiers and civilians—with a concomitant destruction of family and national life. Arguably, the re-evocations of a century past, year by year from 2014 to 2018, unconsciously place us in all manner of affect, nightmares, and reconstructions that profoundly distort our quite modern lives. And perhaps the deluge of remembrance has, at times, led to a turning away from the emotional pain, as being too much to bear, and people retreat instead to a blander life to escape such penetrating evocative accounts of destruction on a massive scale. Perhaps we resist the pull of imagining such sufferings by becoming distant from the news.

Yet, in these last few years we have also seen many collapses in our societies' economic and moral leadership, and the rise of nationalism. Could this be a silent reaction to the too much-ness of the dread of the return of the repressed. Does the emergence of Brexit have a deeper strand of unconscious anxiety: that the UK must free itself from Europe as a bulwark against the Axis powers in the First World War? The end of that war, and how the aftermath was dealt with, was the harbinger of the Second World War a few years later. The rise of the right, the return of the Nazis in many European countries, and increases in anti-Semitism are a return to the legacy of the interwar years. Today, we in Europe and the United States may be unconsciously following a political and immoral lineage from those times just a century ago. If so, we are increasingly involved in emotionally split-off and difficult times. Perhaps the cultural collapses in the First World War have not been mourned sufficiently, so that on the return of its centenary, we are not well protected from the return of its re-evocation. If such a hypothesis is even somewhat correct, it means that we will be living in increasingly difficult times as the years progress, with the previous century's happenings unconsciously returning through to 2045.

At a recent conference in May 2018 titled "Ferenczi in Firenze: Ferenczi in our Times", I was struck with the idea about how he might view our present times. In their voluminous correspondence, he writes to Freud on 29 March 1933 from Budapest:

> Short and sweet: I advise you to make use of the not yet immediately dangerously threatening situation and, with a few patients and your daughter Anna, to go to a more secure country, perhaps England. Levy [his doctor] finds my advice to be much too pessimistic; perhaps he connects it with my generally depressed mood. I, myself, am harbouring the idea, in the event that the political danger gets closer to Budapest, of, at the proper time, going to Switzerland, where some patients who are still capable of paying will accompany me. …Please take my warning seriously.
>
> (Falzeder & Brabant, 2000, pp. 447–8)

Freud writes, in his last ever letter to Ferenczi, on 2 April 1933 from Vienna:

> Now, as concerns the current motive for your writing, the motive of flight, I will gladly inform you that I am not considering leaving Vienna. I am not mobile enough, too dependent on treatment, little alleviations and comforts, also don't like to leave my property in the lurch, but I would probably also remain if I were intact and youthfully fresh. An emotional attitude naturally lies at the base of this decision, but there is also no lack of rationalizations. It is not certain that the Hitler regime will also overpower Austria; it is, of course, possible, but everyone believes that it will not reach the heights of brutality here that it has in Germany. There is certainly no personal danger for me, and if you assume life in oppression to be amply uncomfortable

for us Jews, then don't forget how little contentment life promises refugees in a foreign country, be it Switzerland or England. Flight, I think, would be justified only in the case of lethal danger, and incidentally, if they kill you, it's one kind of death like any other.

(ibid., p. 449)

Ferenczi died on 22 May 1933 of neurological complications of pernicious anaemia (Dupont, 2000, p. xxxviii). Ferenczi, so in touch with the environment of Nazism, is unable to see the imminence of his own death. And Freud, aware of the impact of the Nazis in Germany but not wanting to see them crossing the boundary into Austria. So between these two characters, the individual is left to decide his or her own position. Ferenczi seems to be listening to his own thinking about the environment compared to Freud's belonging to the "everyone believes" category. Today, we are more in need of trying to think for ourselves, despite all the tools available to share and be swallowed up by social media's anodyne offerings.

We may have ahead of us a period of living through in an *après coup* sense, albeit a century later, many of the moments of the war horrors and concentration camp horrors, the latter unknown at that time to Freud and Ferenczi. Yet, this period of time ahead is, in my view, likely to continue to unconsciously destabilise our present lives in Europe, the Middle East, and the US and Russia. Knowing about this potential negative legacy from history may allow us time to know more of the human condition living unconsciously within reminiscences of mourning. Hannah Arendt published *Men in Dark Times* in 1968 as a collection of essays written over the previous decades. She was deeply committed to thinking about the individual's behaviour in dark times. Does one engage in the struggle, or withdraw and use one's limited resources for other matters? Knowledge of such matters that I have attempted to map out, in particular the need for appropriate and sufficient mourning, as well as being aware that it can only be an incomplete task, may help all of us to remember rather than to re-enact the past and, in particular, its many cruelties.

Let this be an appropriate point to end. Attempting to know oneself is central to the ability to shake off the often fool's gold of joining the herd.

References

Abraham, N., & Torok, M. (1994). *The Shell and the Kernel: Renewals of Psychoanalysis*. Chicago: University of Chicago Press.

Akhmatova, A. (1957). *Requiem*. In: P. Forbes (Ed.), *Scanning the Century*. London: Penguin, 1999.

American Psychiatric Association (2013). *Diagnostic and Statistical Manual of Mental Disorders* (5th edn). Washington, DC: American Psychiatric Association.

Arendt, H. (1968). *Men in Dark Times*. New York, NY: Harcourt Brace Jovanovich.

Auestad, L. (2015). *Respect, Plurality, and Prejudice: A Psychoanalytical and Philosophical Enquiry into the Dynamics of Social Exclusion and Discrimination*. London: Karnac.

Benjamin, W. (1933). Experience and poverty (Trans. R. Livingstone). In: M. W. Jennings, M. Bullock, H. Eiland, & G. Smith (Eds.), *Walter Benjamin: Selected Writings 2, 1927–1934* (pp. 731–736). Cambridge, MA: Belknap Press, 2001.

Berenbaum, M. (2001). Why wasn't Auschwitz bombed? In: *Encyclopædia Britannica* <https://www.britannica.com/topic/Why-wasnt-Auschwitz-bombed-717594> (last accessed 8 November 2017).

Bollas, C. (2015). Psychoanalysis in the age of bewilderment: On the return of the oppressed. *International Journal of Psycho-analysis*, *96*: 535–551.

Bratby, R. (2018). "*Metamorphosen*"—*Study for 23 Strings*. Royal Opera House programme, orchestra of the Royal Opera House in concert, Monday 23 April 2018.

Busby, E. (2018, May 9). Government's mental health plans to leave hundreds of thousands of children without needed support, MPs warn. *Independent.* https://www.independent.co.uk/news/education/education-news/childrens-mental-health-government-green-paper-education-select-committee-social-care-a8341821.html (last accessed 19 June 2018).

Connolly, K. (2001, July 11). Poland says sorry for slaughter of Jews. *The Guardian* <https://www.theguardian.com/world/2001/jul/11/poland> (last accessed 12 March 2018).

Dolbear, S., Leslie, E., & Truskolaski, S. (2016). Introduction. In: W. Benjamin, *The Storyteller* (Ed. S. Dolbear, E. Leslie, & S. Truskolaski) (pp. ix–xxxii). London: Verso.

Donald Trump *Access Hollywood* tape (2016). *Washington Post* <https://www.washingtonpost.com/news/the-fix/wp/2016/10/07/the-bush-family-finally-does-some-damage-to-donald-trumps-campaign-via-an-unlikely-bush/> (last accessed 23 March 2018).

Dupont, J. (2000). Introduction. In: E. Falzeder & E. Brabant (Eds.), *The Correspondence of Sigmund Freud and Sándor Ferenczi, Volume 3: 1920–1933* (pp. xvii–xi). Cambridge, MA: Belknap.

Falzeder, E. & Brabant, E. (Eds.) (2000). *The Correspondence of Sigmund Freud and Sándor Ferenczi, Volume 3: 1920–1933.* Translated by P. T. Hoffer. Cambridge, MA: Belknap.

Fanon, F. (1952). *Black Skin, White Masks* (Trans. R. Philcox). New York: Grove Press, 2008.

Ferenczi, S. (1933). Confusion of tongues between adults and the child. In: M. Balint (Ed.), *Final Contributions to the Problems and Methods of Psychoanalysis* (pp. 156–167). London: Hogarth, 1955.

Flood, A. (2014, November 12). Grimm brothers' fairytales have blood and horror restored in new translation. *The Guardian* <www.theguardian.com/books/2014/nov/12/grimm-brothers-fairytales-horror-new-translation> (last accessed 27 October 2017).

Forrester, K. (2015, October 22). Don't join a union, pop a pill. *London Review of Books* <www.lrb.co.uk/v37/n20/katrina-forrester/dont-join-a-union-pop-a-pill> (last accessed 27 October 2017).

Foy, H. (2015, November 20). The lost faces of Lublin. *The Financial Times* <www.ft.com/content/3045ba30-8e34-11e5-8be4-3506bf20cc2b?mhq5j=e7> (last accessed 19 October 2017).

Freedland, J. (2015, December 10). The day Israel saw Shoah. *The Guardian* <www.theguardian.com/world/2015/dec/10/the-day-israel-saw-shoah> (last accessed 19 October 2017).

Freud, A. (1936). *The Ego and the Mechanisms of Defence*. London: Karnac, 1992.

Freud, S. (1905a). *Jokes and Their Relation to the Unconscious. S.E., 8*. London: Hogarth.

Freud, S. (1919e). "A child is being beaten": A contribution to the study of the origin of sexual perversions. *S.E., 17*: 175–204. London: Hogarth.

Freud, S. (1920g). Beyond the pleasure principle. *S.E., 18*: 1–64. London: Hogarth.

Freud, S. (1921c). Group psychology and the analysis of the ego. *S.E., 18*: 65–144. London: Hogarth.

Freud, S. (1923, March 4). Letter to Romain Rolland. In: E. Freud (Ed.), *Letters of S. Freud, 1873–1939* (p. 346). London: Hogarth, 1961.

Freud, S. (1924). Neurosis and psychosis. *S.E., 19*: 147–154.

Freud, S. (1925a). A note upon the "mystic writing pad". *S.E., 19*: 227–232. London: Hogarth.

Freud, S. (1925d). An autobiographical study. *S.E., 20*: 1–74. London: Hogarth.

Freud, S. (1939a). *Moses and Monotheism: Three Essays. S.E., 23*: 1–138.

Goldhagen, D. J. (1996). *Hitler's Willing Executioners: Ordinary Germans and the Holocaust*. London: Abacus.

Grimm, J., & Grimm, W. (1812). *The Original Folk and Fairy Tales of the Brothers Grimm: The Complete First Edition* (Trans. & Ed. J. Zipes). Woodstock: Princeton University Press, 2014.

Gross, J. T. (2000). *Neighbors: The Destruction of the Jewish Community in Jedwabne, Poland*. London: Arrow Books, 2003.

Grossman, D. (2012). D. Grossman interview with D. Aaronovitch. In: *Hay Festival Conversations: Thirty Conversations for Thirty Years* (pp. 109–115). Hay: Hay Festival Press, 2017.

Guilford, G. (2016, April 1). Inside the Trump machine: The bizarre psychology of America's newest political movement. *Quartz* <https://qz.com/645345/inside-the-trump-machine-the-bizarre-psychology-of-americas-newest-political-movement/> (last accessed 9 March 2018).

Heaney, S. (1995). Nobel lecture, 7 December 1995. *Nobelprize.org* <https://www.nobelprize.org/nobel_prizes/literature/laureates/1995/heaney-lecture.html> [last accessed 19 April 2018].

Kaeser, J. (2018, May 20). Fears over far-right prompt Siemens chief to rebuke AfD politician. *Financial Times* <https://www.ft.com/content/046821ba-5c17-11e8-9334-2218e7146b04> (last accessed 5 July 2018).

Kafka, F. (1919). Letter to his father. Quoted in: R. Stach, *Kafka: The Early Years* (p. 65). Princeton: Princeton University Press, 2017.

Kermode, F. (2000). *The Sense of an Ending: Studies in the Theory of Fiction with a New Epilogue*. Oxford: Oxford University Press.

The Kielce Pogram: A Blood Libel Massacre of Holocaust Survivors. In: *Holocaust Ency-clopedia* <https://www.ushmm.org/wlc/en/article.php?ModuleId=10007941> (last accessed 1 March 2018).

Kizilhan, J. (2014, August 15). Isis betrieben Genozid auf Raten. *Bild* <http://www.bild.de/politik/ausland/jesiden/gastkommentar-jesiden-37261394.bild.html> (last accessed 9 November 2017).

Klemperer, V. (1957). *The Language of the Third Reich*. London: Bloomsbury, 2013.

Lanzmann, C. (Dir.) (1985). *Shoah*. New Yorker Films.

Levi, P. (1959). *If This is a Man*. London: Vintage, 1996.

Major, R., & Talagrand, C. (2018). *Freud: The Unconscious and World Affairs* (Trans. A. Jacob). London: Routledge.

Marija Vezmar, M. (2018, April). Personal communication.

Mills, C. (2003). Introduction. In: C. Mills & P. H. Simpson (Eds.), *Monuments to the Lost Cause: Women, Art, and the Landscapes of Southern Memory* (pp. xv–xxx). Knoxville: University of Tennessee Press.

Mitscherlich, A., & Mielke, F. (1949). *Doctors of Infamy: The Story of the Nazi Medi-cal Crimes* (Trans. H. Norden). New York: Schuman.

Mitscherlich, A., & Mitscherlich, M. (1967). *The Inability to Mourn: Principles of Collective Behavior*. New York: Random House, 1975.

Mohdin, A. (2017, September 17). How Germany took in one million refugees but dodged a populist uprising. *Quartz* <https://qz.com/1076820/german-election-how-angela-merkel-took-in-one-million-refugees-and-avoided-a-populist-upset/> (last accessed 12 March 2018).

Molnar, M. (Ed.) (1992). *The Diary of Sigmund Freud: 1929–1939: A Record of the Final Decade*. New York: Scribner's.

Money-Kyrle, R. (1941). The psychology of propaganda. In: D. Meltzer & E. O'Shaughnessy (Eds.), *The Collected Papers of Roger Money-Kyrle* (pp. 160–175). London: Karnac on behalf of the Harris Meltzer Trust, 2015.

Morrison, T. (2017). *The Origin of Others*. Cambridge, MA: Harvard University Press.

Novick, J., & Novick, K. (1997). Not for barbarians: An appreciation of Freud's "A child is being beaten". In: E. S. Person (Ed.), *On Freud's "A Child Is Being Beaten"* (pp. 31–46). London: Karnac.

Peck, R. (Dir.) (2016). *I Am Not Your Negro*. Magnolia Pictures.

Poland's holocaust law has worrying echoes (2018, February 9). *The Financial Times* <https://www.ft.com/content/ccaf3370-0da7-11e8-8eb7-42f857ea9f09> (last accessed 1 March 2018).

Roberts, S. (2016, July 5). Off the beaten track in Ethiopia. *The Financial Times* <https://howtospendit.ft.com/travel/109543-a-luxury-four-bedroom-villa-escape-in-the-himalayas> (last accessed 21 October 2017).

Rolnik, E. J. (2012). *Freud in Zion: Psychoanalysis and the Making of Modern Jewish Identity*. London: Karnac.

Sands, P. (2016, April 15). On genocide and trauma. *The Financial Times* <www.ft.com/content/2ce55dee-01c7-11e6-ac98-3c15a1aa2e62?mhq5j=e7> (last accessed 17 October 2017).

Sands, P. (2017, April 22). Primo Levi's *If This Is a Man* at 70. *The Guardian* <www.theguardian.com/books/2017/apr/22/primo-levi-auschwitz-if-this-is-a-man-memoir-70-years> (last accessed 27 October 2017).

Shore, M. (2018, February 4). Poland digs itself a memory hole. *The New York Times* <https://www.nytimes.com/2018/02/04/opinion/poland-holocaust-law-justice-government.html> (last accessed 28 February 2018).

Sklar, J. (2011). *Landscapes of the Dark: History, Trauma, Psychoanalysis*. London: Karnac.

Sklar, J. (2017). *Balint Matters: Psychosomatics and the Art of Assessment*. London: Karnac.

Stach, R. (2017). *Kafka: The Early Years*. Princeton: Princeton University Press.

Stevenson, B. (2017, July 13). A presumption of guilt. *The New York Review of Books* <http://www.nybooks.com/articles/2017/07/13/presumption-of-guilt/> (last accessed 10 November 2017).

Tutu, D. M. (1999). *No Future Without Forgiveness*. London: Rider, 2000.

Varoufakis, Y. (2016). *And the Weak Suffer What They Must*. London: Bodley Head.

Wilson, J., Helmore, E., & Swain, J. (2017, August 13). Man charged with murder after driving into anti-far-right protesters in Charlottesville. *The Guardian*. https://www.theguardian.com/us-news/2017/aug/12/virginia-unite-the-right-rally-protest-violence (last accessed 03/07/2018).

Winnicott, D. W. (1947). Hate in the countertransference. In: *Through Paediatrics to Psycho-analysis* (pp. 194–203). London: Hogarth, 1975.

Yang, Y. (2018, April 18). The quiet revolution: China's millennial backlash. *Financial Times* <https://www.ft.com/content/dae2c548-4226-11e8-93cf-67ac3a6482fd> [last accessed 23 April 2018].

Young, J. E. (1993). *The Texture of Memory: Holocaust Memorials and Meaning*. New Haven: Yale University Press.

Žižek, S. (1993). *Tarrying with the Negative*. Durham, NC: Duke University Press.

Index

Abraham, Nicholas, 28
abuse *see* aggressor, identification with;
    child abuse
activism, 53, 73, 78
    see also protests; revolution; strike
      action
aggressor, identification with, 18, 48, 54,
    56, 58, 60, 62, 65
Akhmatova, Anna, 1, 15–16
alcoholism, 35
    see also drug abuse
aliveness, 13, 24, 30, 31, 42, 60
    see also freedom; dissonance
Allies, 26–27, 35–36, 38, 39, 75
anti-Semitism of, 36
alt-right, 20, 32, 61, 64
alterity *see* the other
analyst
    death of, 23
    freedom of, 2, 13
    history of, 5
    role of in therapy, 12–13, 16, 22, 50
    see also psychoanalysis
anti-fascism, ix–x, 19, 68, 74

see also fascism *and under*
    Communism
anti-Semitism
    as biphasic attack, 18, 20
    countering, ix–x, 19
    effect on family, 54, 64
    instrumentalising of, 19–20
    Islamist, 19
    pogroms, ix, xx, 43–44, 64
    today, 19–20, 22, 68, 70–71, 76
    unconscious, 37
    in United Kingdom, ix
    see also Holocaust; Jews; *and under*
      Allies; Communism; Freud,
      Sigmund; Nazi Germany;
      psychoanalysis; Poland; United
      States
après coup, 24, 42, 49, 78
architecture, 13–14, 39, 51
    see also memorials
Arendt, Hannah, 78
art, 71, 72
    see also creativity
asylum, 25, 31–32, 41, 47, 78

see also immigration; migration;
    refugees
austerity politics, 12
    see also economics, right-wing;
        inequality

Baldwin, James, 62, 65, 66
Baldwin, Stanley, ix
Balint, Michael, 10, 40
    see also new beginnings
Benjamin, Walter, 26, 49, 50
Black Lives Matter, 73, 74
Bluebeard, 28
Boehm, Felix, 6, 7
Bollas, Christopher, 67
    see also horizontalism
Bonaparte, Princess Marie, xx
Brexit, 1, 12, 36, 42, 76
Buckley Jr, William, 62
Busby, Eleanor, 2

Cameron, David, 12
Canaletto, 14
capitalism, 22, 29, 30
    see also economics, right-wing
Ceauşescu, Nicholae, 41
censorship, 7, 15, 27, 29, 36
    see also under truth
child abuse, 28, 47, 51, 55, 56
    Ferenczi on, 17–18
    inflicted by ISIS, 31, 32, 33
    relation to aggression towards the
        other, 54, 60, 61, 62
    see also aggressor, identification
        with
China, xix
Chodakiewicz, Marek, 44
Churchill, Winston, 26, 35
climate change, 42
cognitive-behavioural therapy, 4
Cold War, 27, 38
colonialism, 50
Communism
    and anti-fascism, ix
    anti-Semitism under, 33–34, 43
    collapse of, 9, 22, 41

control systems of, 5, 9, 22, 41, 42
International Brigade, ix–x
as Jewish plot, 39
as other, 3, 21, 38–39
    see also Eastern Bloc; Germany;
        USSR; totalitarianism
conformity, *see* psychological
        manipulation *and under*
        freedom *and* society
contrapuntal listening, 9, 10, 11
creativity, 9, 67, 42
    see also art; dissonance; music;
        nursery rhymes; stories;
        writing; *and under* freedom

death, 23, 26, 58
    see also mourning
death drive, 58, 74
death penalty, 64
defence mechanisms *see* splits/splitting
delusion *see* patch
democracy, ix, 49, 51, 71
    see also totalitarianism
denial, 28, 42, 71
    see also post-truth politics;
        repression; splits/splitting;
        and under mourning; Nazi
        Germany; Holocaust; truth
*Diagnostic and Statistical Manual of
    Medical Disorders*, 30
    see also psychiatry
Dolbear, Sam, 26
dissonance, 16, 23
domination, *see* master–slave mentality;
        totalitarianism; *and under*
        family; freedom
dreams, 41, 44–45
drug abuse, 60, 61
    see also alcoholism; pharmaceutics
Duda, Andrzej, 27, 42

early environment *see* child abuse; family
Eastern Bloc, 1, 5, 22, 38–39
    see also Cold War; Communism;
        Poland; Romania; Serbia;
        USSR; *and under* Germany

economics, right-wing, 22, 47
    see also austerity politics; capitalism;
        inequality
ego *see under* gap; splits/splitting; tears
Egypt, 50
Eisenman, Peter, 15
Eitingon, Max, 6
elasticity, 11, 12
empathy, 37
endings, 16, 17, 21, 23, 76
    see also death; loss; mourning
Enlightenment, 50–51
equality, 49, 66, 69
    see also inequality
Ethiopia, 49
Europe
    aggression of/in, 2–3, 12, 14–15
    European Court of Justice, 4
    European Convention of Human
        Rights, 4
    European Psychoanalytic Congress,
        43
    European Psychoanalytical
        Federation, 7, 9, 10, 13
    European Union, 3–4, 12
    heterogeneity of, 8, 13
    history of, 2, 3, 8, 13, 14–15
    need for equality in, 49
    see also Brexit; Eastern Bloc; France;
        Nazi Germany; Poland;
        Romania; Serbia; Spain; United
        Kingdom; USSR; *and under*
        Holocaust; immigration;
        psychoanalytic societies;
        repetition

Facebook *see* social media
fake news, xviii, 30, 71, 73
    see also post-truth politics
family
    abuse in, xvii
    atmosphere in, xvii, 65
    dominance and passivity in, 16, 22,
        54, 55, 66, 67
    dominant narrative in, 16
    hate in, 61, 65

"normality" of, 65
    violence in, 28, 54
    see also aggressor, identification
        with; father; good-enough;
        mother; parent; *and under*
        anti-Semitism; racism
Fanon, Frantz, 65
fascism, ix–x, xvi, 1, 45–46, 68
    see also anti-fascism; anti-Semitism;
        nationalism; Nazi Germany;
        Nazism; totalitarianism
father, 55–59 *passim*, 68
    see also family; mother; parent; *and
        under* leader
feminism, xvii
    see also misogyny; women's rights
Ferenczi, Sandor
    "Confusion of Tongues between
        Adults and the Child", 17, 18,
        28, 47
    and Freud, 17, 77–78
    life of, 77–78
    see also elasticity *and under* child
        abuse
First World War, 3, 25, 26, 42, 45, 58
    centenary of, 76, 77
Forrester, Katrina, 29
Foster, Norman, 51
Foy, Henry, 33
France
    Charlie Hebdo shooting, 19–20
    French Revolution, 64
    Front National, 21
    Institute of France, 50
    Rassemblement National, 21
    see also Napoleon *and under* Jews
Franco, Francisco, x
free association, 10, 11, 16, 22, 24,
    69–70
Freedland, Jonathan, 35
freedom
    through creativity, 25, 57, 58, 60
    of individual within society,
        xvi–xvii, xxi, 2, 8, 24, 32, 78
    deprivation of, 43, 49, 57–58, 71
    under totalitarianism, xix, 16, 58

of therapy, 2, 5, 16, 22, 24;
  negation of, 10
  through therapy, 12, 13, 16, 21–22,
    24, 50
  see also aliveness; dissonance;
    domination; free association;
    revolution; totalitarianism; and
    under language; society
Freud, Anna, 18
Freud, Sigmund
  anti-Semitism of, 8
  on anti-Semitism, xx, 7
  "An Autobiographical Study", xv
  "Beyond the Pleasure Principle",
    44–45
  censorship of, 7, 15, 36
  "A Child Is Being Beaten", 55, 58, 59
  Civilization and Its Discontents, 43
  fears for psychoanalysis, 4, 36
  and Ferenczi, 17, 77–78
  "Group Psychology and the
    Analysis of the Ego", 58
  and irony, xix
  Jokes and Their Relation to the
    Unconscious, xviii
  letter to Ernest Jones, 6
  letter to Romain Rolland, 7
  life of, xx, 3, 58, 77
  Moses and Monotheism, xx, 7
  "Neurosis and Psychosis", 14, 40
  "A Note upon the 'Mystic Writing
    Pad'", xvi
  as witness to Nazism, xix–xx, 3, 7,
    36, 77–78
fundamentalism, 31, 32, 48, 51, 66
  see also Isis and Islamism

gaps
  in ego, 40, 47
  as healthy, 42
  in society, 7, 39, 40, 41–42, 47, 48
  see also patch; splits/splitting; tear
genocide, 31, 32–33
  see also Holocaust
Germany
  Alternative for Germany Party, xvi

Berlin Psychoanalytic Institute,
  6, 7, 11
Berlin Wall:
  fall of, xvi–xvii, 8, 22, 30, 39
  psychological impact of, xvi–xvii
  division/unification of, xvi–xvii, 8,
    22, 38–39, 51
  German Medical Society, 15
  memorials in, 15, 70, 73
  Munich National Theatre, 75
  Reichstag, 39, 51
  Siemens, xvi
  treatment of refugees in, 31–32,
    34, 48
  xenophobia in, 34, 48
  see also Hitler, Adolf; Nazi
    Germany
ghettoisation, 64–65
globalisation, 67
  see also internationalism
Goebbels, Joseph, 45
Goethe, Johann Wolfgang von, 75, 76
Gone with the Wind, 72
good-enough, 48, 54, 56, 60, 61, 65
  see also Winnicott, Donald
Google, 29–30
Göring, Matthias, 6
Grimms' Fairy Tales, 28–29
Gross, Jan Tomasz, 43, 44
Grossman, David, 25
group dynamics, 20–21, 60, 78
  us vs them, 20–21, 30, 39, 45, 46, 53,
    54, 60, 62
    countering, 49, 78
    as nationalism, 3
    as racism, 62, 65–66
    as religious identity, 19
    as sadism, 34
    unconscious, 54, 69
  see also Holocaust; homophobia;
    Islamophobia; misogyny;
    nationalism; the other; racism;
    refugees; splits/splitting;
    transphobia; xenophobia
Guilford, Gwynn, 46
guilt, 22, 55, 60

hate, 36, 48
    in society, 54, 55, 64
    unconscious, 40, 64
    see also under the other; family;
        parent
haunting, 16, 22, 40, 61, 74
Heaney, Seamus, 11
Heine, Heinrich, 15
history *see* time *and under* Europe;
    immigration; psychoanalysis;
    repression; trauma; truth
Hitchcock, Alfred, 26–27
Hitler, Adolf, xx, 30, 38, 39, 45–46
    see also leader *and under* Trump,
        Donald
Holocaust, ixx–xx
    acknowledgement/mourning of,
        8, 15, 26–27, 33–36 *passim*,
        70, 73
    denial or avoidance of, 7, 14,
        15, 27, 29–30, 38, 42–44, 70–71
    concentration camps, xix, 2, 3, 15,
        31, 33, 43, 73
        Auschwitz, xix, 35, 36, 44, 70
        Birkenau, 35–36
        documenting of, 26–27
        non-bombing of, 35–36
    as European project, 2, 20, 36
    in terms of group dynamics, 21
    Holocaust Memorial Day, 21
    Shoah, 35, 49
    and Siemens, xvi
    survivors of, 33, 35, 43–44
    see also anti-Semitism; genocide;
        Nazi Germany; *Shoah; and
        under* memorials; Poland
homophobia, 18–19
hope, xvii, 17, 32, 60, 61
horizontalism, 67–68, 69
Horkheimer, Max, 49
human rights *see under* Europe

I Am Not Your Negro, 62
immigration
    and Europe today, 1, 34, 41–42
    history of within Europe, ix, 3, 44

    see also asylum; migration; refugees;
        xenophobia
inequality, 20, 22, 47, 66
    see also austerity politics; economics,
        right-wing; equality
International Psychoanalytical
    Association, 23
internationalism, 53
    see also globalisation
internet, 67
    see also Google; social media
Iraq, 31, 32
irony, xviii, xix
    see also language
Isis, 30–31, 32, 51
    see also Islamism; terrorism; *and
        under* child abuse
Islam, 50–51
    see also Islamism; Islamophobia
Islamism, 19, 30–31, 32, 51
    see also Isis; Islam; terrorism
Islamophobia, xvi, 18, 19, 46, 54, 62
Israel, 20–21, 35

Jefferson, Thomas, 66
Jews
    Association of Jewish
        Ex-Servicemen, ix
    in France, 19
    in Poland, 13, 33, 34, 35, 40, 44
    shtetl Jews, ix, 3, 64
    in Spain, 14–15
    in United Kingdom, ix
    see also anti-Semitism;
        Holocaust; Israel; *and under*
        psychoanalysis
Jones, Ernest, 6
journalism, 19, 29, 30, 46–47, 76
    see also fake news
justice, 3–4, 11, 32–33, 38
    lack of, 62, 63, 64
    see also law; revenge; *and under*
        Nazi Germany

Kaeser, Joe, xvi
Kafka, Franz, 56, 57, 58, 62

Kermode, Frank, 21, 23
Kizilhan, Jan, 30–32, 34
Klein, Melanie, 59
Klemperer, Victor, xxi
Kwaśniewski, President Aleksander, 44

Lampl-de Groot, Jeanne, xx
language, xviii–xix, xxi, 11–12, 21
    see also irony and writing
Lanzmann, Claude, 35, 49
law, x, xix, 42–43, 50, 54, 57, 58, 60, 63,
        64, 71–72
    see also justice; women's rights; and
        under Europe; United States
leader
    aggression of, 54, 58, 60, 61, 68
    death of, 39
    double embodiment of, 39
    idolisation of leader, 30, 38, 46, 68;
        as father, 58, 68
    projection into, 54, 58, 60, 61
    tyrannical, 71
    weak, 42, 76
    see also Ceauşescu, Nicholae; Hitler,
        Adolf; Trump, Donald
Le Pen, Marine, 21
Lee, Robert E., 74
Leslie, Esther, 26
Levi, Primo, 53
listening, see contrapuntal listening; free
        association; elasticity; stories;
        and under the other
loss, 37–38, 47, 70, 71
    see also mourning
love
    and melancholia, 38
    and mourning, 37
    and parent, 47, 55, 56, 65, 66
lying see post-truth politics; truth

Major, René, xviii–xx
masochism, 33, 55, 56, 58, 59, 60
    see also sadism; sadomasochism
master–slave mentality, 11, 12
May, Theresa, 53
melancholia, 37, 38, 42, 46

memorials
    to book-burning, 15, 70
    to Confederate States of America,
        71, 72, 73
    to Holocaust, 15, 33, 34, 36, 49, 70,
        73
    to lynchings, 73–74
    to war, 76
    see also mourning
Mengele, Dr Josef, 15
Merkel, Angela, 31–32
Mielke, Fred, 15
migration see immigration; refugees
Mills, Cynthia, 71
mindfulness, 28
misogyny, xvii, 31, 32, 43, 46, 54, 59
    see also rape; women's rights
Mitscherlich, Alexander, 15, 38
Mitscherlich-Nielsen, Margarete, 15, 38
Mohammed, 50–51
Molnar, Michael, xx
Money-Kyrle, Roger, 45
monuments, see architecture; memorials
Morrison, Toni, 66
Mosley, Sir Oswald, ix, x
mother, 9–10, 58–59, 60, 61, 65, 73
    see also family; father; parent
mourning, 25
    difference to melancholia, 37–38
    false, 13
    importance of, 30
    lack/elision of, 13, 14, 15, 27, 30, 38,
        62, 70, 77
    of historical trauma, 8, 12, 15, 17, 37,
        40, 73–78 passim; of Holocaust,
        33–36 passim, 49, 70
    in parent–child relationship, 12,
        73–74
    in psychoanalytic societies, 13
    see also death; endings; loss;
        memorials; and under
        architecture
Mugabe, Robert, xvi
Müller-Braunschweig, Carl, 7
music, 9, 16, 75–76
    see also creativity

Nachträglichkeit, 24, 42
Napoleon, 50
narcissism, 9, 38, 67
nationalism, 3, 44, 53, 76
    see also fascism; xenophobia; *and*
        under group dynamics
Nazi Germany, ixx–xx
    Allied bombing of, 75
    anti-Semitism of, xv–xvi, xix–xx,
        6–7, 45, 66, 76
    and censorship, 7, 15, 36
    citizens of, 27, 39
    collapse of, 39
    control systems of, 5
    crimes of, 42; medical, 15
    and dehumanisation of other, 32
    German Institute for Psychological
        Research and Psychotherapy,
        6–7
    historical acknowledgement of, 15,
        73–74
        suppression or denial of, 15,
            27, 29–30, 38, 70–71
        and language, xxi
    League of German Girls, xvi
    prosecution of Nazi criminals, 38
    psychological legacy of, 7, 8
    racist beliefs of, 38
    rallies, 30, 45, 46
    return of, 48
    see also Hitler, Adolf; Holocaust;
        Nazism; totalitarianism;
        Untermenschen; *and under*
        Freud, Sigmund; Poland;
        psychoanalysis; psychoanalytic
        societies; racism
Nazism
    as barbarism, 7
    neo-, 8, 20, 21, 32, 48, 60, 62, 64,
        67–68, 70–71, 73, 74, 76
    see also Nazi Germany;
        Rassemblement National; *and*
        under France; Poland; racism
neoliberalism *see* capitalism; economics,
        right-wing
Netanyahu, Benjamin, 19–20

new beginnings, 10, 12–13, 24, 40, 50
news *see* fake news; journalism
NHS, 2, 4, 12
Night Will Fall, 27
Novick, Jack, 55, 58
Novick, Kerry, 55, 58
nursery rhymes, 59–60

Oedipus, xx
oedipal, 17, 55, 58, 59
    pre-, 17
oration, 30, 45–46
Orwell, George, 11
the other
    big Other, 41
    dehumanisation of, 21, 32
    listening to, 9, 10, 11, 49
    meaningfulness of alterity, 9, 67
    prejudice, hatred, aggression
        towards, 27, 37, 41, 45, 61, 64
        comparison with biphasic
            attack in child abuse, 18, 19, 20
        countering, 9, 36, 64
        in divided Germany, 39
        by Donald Trump, 20, 46,
            60–61, 64
        nationalism as, 3, 39
        in Nazi Germany, 46
        relation to abuse, 60, 61, 62, 65
        as social control, 5, 26, 46, 64, 68
    projecting blame onto, 1, 22, 37, 45,
        48, 54, 65
        in Nazi Germany, 46
        by Donald Trump, 20
        resisting, 36
    see also anti-Semitism; group
        dynamics; homophobia;
        Islamophobia; misogyny;
        nationalism; racism; refugees;
        transphobia; *ubuntu*;
        xenophobia; *and under* child
        abuse; Communism; Trump,
        Donald

paedophilia *see* aggressor, identification
        with; child abuse

paranoia, 5–6, 12, 22, 39, 41, 46
parent
    authority of, 22
    domination by, 54, 66
    identification with, 54
    and love, 47, 55, 56, 66–67
        lack of, 48, 68
    narcissism of, 67
    parent–child relationship, xvii, 61
        hate in, 45, 59–62 *passim*, 65
    weakness of, 65
    see also family; father; mother
patch, 14, 24, 39, 40, 41
    see also gaps
patriarchy, xvii
    see also misogyny
Peck, Raoul, 62
pharmaceutics, 30
Pietrasiewicz, Tomasz, 33, 34
play *see* creativity
Poland
    anti-Semitism in, ix, 7, 8, 33–34,
        43–44
        pogroms, 43–44
    and the Holocaust, 7, 8, 13–14, 27,
        33, 34, 35, 42, 43
        Auschwitz, xix, 35, 36, 70
        Birkenau, 35–36
        Majdanek, 33
    Law and Justice party, 7, 27, 42–43
    Lublin and Grodzka Gate NN
        Theatre, 33, 34, 36, 40, 49
    Nazi occupation of, 13–14, 27,
        42, 43
    Polish Centre for Holocaust
        Research, 43
    Polish resistance, 13–14
    psychoanalysis in, 7, 8, 43
    Warsaw: ghetto, 8, 13–14, 25, 35
        Jewish uprising in, 13, 35
        mourning in, 13
        reconstruction of, 14
    see also under Jews; Trump, Donald
police, ix, x, 44, 72, 74
Pompeii, 28
post-truth politics
    as denial, 28

historical, 26–27, 45–46
today, 1, 12, 20, 29–30, 67, 70–71
see also fake news; horizontalism;
    truth; *and under* Trump,
    Donald
poverty *see* austerity politics; economics,
    right-wing; inequality; *and*
    under Freud
prejudice *see under* the other;
    psychoanalytic societies
projection *see under* leader; the other;
    racism
propaganda *see* post-truth politics
protests, ix–x, 27, 68, 74
    see also activism; revolution; strike
        action
psychiatry, 30
    see also cognitive-behavioural
        therapy
psychoanalysis
    and anti-Semitism, 8
    and historical trauma, 13, 22
    of history and society, xv, xvi, xvii,
        xx, 3, 8, 36–37, 50, 58
    hostility towards, 2, 4, 5, 6–7
    in Nazi Germany, 6–7
    perception of as a Jewish science,
        xv–xvi, 4, 6, 7, 8
    use against aggression/domination
        in society, x, xvi, 8, 12, 22, 30,
        36, 50, 69–70
    see also analyst *and under* freedom;
        Freud, Sigmund; Poland;
        totalitarianism; truth
psychoanalytic societies
    conferences, 7–8, 68–70, 77
    as control systems, 5, 10
    in Europe today, 7–9, 10, 77
    and historical trauma, 5, 6, 13, 22
    and negotiating difference, 9, 10, 13
    prejudice within, 4, 9, 11, 13
    and trauma within, 13
    see also International
        Psychoanalytical Association;
        Vienna Psychoanalytic Society;
        and under Europe; Germany;
        mourning; Nazi Germany

psychological manipulation, 26, 29, 30, 68
psychosis, 14, 40, 46
psychosomatics, xxi, 47, 56, 60

racism
    as biphasic attack, 18–19, 20
    child's non-understanding of, 64–65
    countering, 69–70, 73
    effect on family, 54, 64, 65
    of family, 65, 66
    and murder, 71–72, 73
    of Nazism, 38
    as projective, 20, 26, 37, 38, 54, 62, 65–66, 69
    pseudoscientific, 66
    systematic, 64, 71–72
    trope of black men raping white women, 71–72
    unconscious, 37, 66, 69, 71
    see also anti-Semitism; Black Lives Matter; ghettoisation; Holocaust; Islamophobia; Nazism; Nazi Germany; South Africa; xenophobia; and under family; group dynamics; the other; Trump, Donald; United States
rape, 31, 32, 71
    see also child abuse; misogyny
reconciliation, 49, 73, 74
    see also under South Africa
refugees
    care for, 31–32, 47, 48
    fleeing racial terrorism, 63
    hate towards, xvi, 41, 48
    Yazidi, 31–32
    see also asylum; immigration; xenophobia
religion see fundamentalism; Islam; Islamism; and under split/splitting
repetition
    of history, 44–45, 76–78
        in Europe, x, xvi, 4, 21, 39–40, 76–78
        of racism in the United States, 72

    by individual, 24, 44–45, 50
repression
    of historical trauma, x, 5, 8, 14, 15, 16, 26, 27, 38, 39, 40, 49, 70, 73, 76–77
    of personal trauma, 14, 16, 26, 28, 40, 49
    return of repressed, x, 4, 21, 44, 72, 76, 77, 78
    of social violence and oppression, xvi, 4, 21, 29, 71
    see also censorship; haunting; repetition; and under Holocaust; Nazi Germany; truth
revenge, 54, 56, 62, 72
    see also justice
revolution, 39, 41, 64
    see also activism; protests
Rolland, Romain, 7
Rolnik, Eran J., 6, 7
Roman Empire, 64
Romania, 41
Russia see USSR

sadism, 33, 34, 47, 55, 56, 60, 62, 74
    see also aggressor, identification with; masochism; sadomasochism
sadomasochism, 33, 36, 47, 54, 55, 56, 59
    see also aggressor, identification with; masochism; sadism
Said, Edward, 9
Sands, Philippe, 31, 53
Second World War, 14, 25, 35–36, 75, 76
    see also Allies; Holocaust; Nazi Germany; and under Poland
Serbia, x, 19
shit, 21, 46, 69
Shore, Marci, 27, 43
Sklar, Jonathan, 8, 13, 68
    Balint Matters, 74
    Landscapes of the Dark, 40
slavery, 31, 63, 64, 66, 71, 72
Smith, David Livingstone, 46
social media, 27, 29, 30, 47, 68, 78

society
    and conformity, 16, 21
    relation of individual psychology to,
        3, 16, 45, 54
    unconscious of, 45
    and see under hate; psychoanalysis;
        splits/splitting; truth
Solms, Mark, 68
South Africa, 5, 68–69
    truth and reconciliation, 6, 37
    see also *ubuntu*
Spain
    Spanish Civil War, ix–x
    Spanish Inquisition, 64
    see also under Jews
splits/splitting
    in ego, 17, 18, 28, 40–41, 47
    religious, 31, 51
    in society, xvii, 19, 20, 30, 36, 37, 38,
        39, 48, 49, 60, 77
        countering of, 51
    see also gaps; patch; tears; walls as
        metaphors; *and under* group
        dynamics
Stach, Reiner, 57
Stevenson, Bryan, 63, 64, 65
stories
    and aliveness, 25
    and everyday life, 27, 46–47, 68–71
    intergenerational, 50
    lost, 49
    sanitising of, 28–29, 36–37
    and trauma, 26, 30, 33, 34, 49
    see also creativity; writing; *and*
        under truth *and* Holocaust
Strauss, Richard, 75, 76
strike action, ix
    see also activism; protests
surveillance, 5, 6, 12, 22, 29, 30
    see also totalitarianism

Talagrand, Chantal, xviii–xx
tears
    in body, 47
    psychic, 40–41, 47

in society, 14, 47, 48
    see also gaps; patch; splits/splitting
terrorism, 1, 19, 20, 63, 64, 65, 73
    see also Isis
time, 23–24
    see also endings
Torok, Maria, 28
totalitarianism, xvi
    countering of, xxi, 8, 30, 53, 57, 68
    and hatred of psychoanalysis, 30
    and language, xviii–xix, xxi, 11–12
    and "ordinary sensible" paranoia, 5
    return of, 8, 20, 22, 39–40, 43, 54,
        60, 68, 71, 76–77
    social and psychological effects of,
        5, 6, 7, 12, 22
    in USSR, 1, 22
    see also leader; Nazi Germany;
        psychological manipulation;
        revolution; surveillance;
        Trump, Donald; *and under*
        Communism; freedom
trade unions, ix
transference, 2, 4, 5, 10, 36
transphobia, 54
trauma
    compounding of, 20
    generational, 3, 9, 61
    interface between personal and
        historical, 3, 5, 6, 8, 22, 35,
        58, 74
    treatment of victims, 31, 32, 33
    see also anti-Semitism; child abuse;
        First World War; Holocaust;
        ISIS; misogyny; racism; Second
        World War; Yazidi; *and under*
        mourning; psychoanalysis;
        psychoanalytic societies;
        repression
Trump, Donald
    Access Hollywood tape, xvii
    attacks on the other, 20, 36, 42, 46,
        54, 60–61
    comparisons with Hitler, 39, 46
    misogyny of, xvii

and Poland, 44
post-truth politics of, xvii, 27,
    68, 71
racism of, 20, 46, 53, 60, 61, 64,
    67–68, 73
rallies, 30
as totalitarian, 20, 27, 54, 61,
    68, 71
see also leader; post-truth politics
Truskolaski, Samuel, 26
trust, 11, 13, 17, 18, 19, 22, 69
truth
    asserting of, 11, 75, 78
        in face of suppression, xix
        historical, 6, 49, 70, 78
        and psychoanalysis, 12
        of society, 68–70
    avoidance/suppression of, 21, 29,
        71, 76, 77–78
        in attacks on alterity, 18–19
        in child abuse, 18
    documenting of, 26–27, 33, 34, 35,
        36, 49, 73
    see also censorship; denial;
        freedom; memorials;
        mourning; post-truth politics;
        repression; stories; writing;
        and under Holocaust; Nazi
        Germany; South Africa;
        United States
Tutu, Desmond, 37
Twitter *see* social media

ubuntu, 37, 69–70
Ullman, Micha, 15
United Kingdom, ix, x
    see also Brexit; Cameron, David;
        May, Theresa; NHS; *and under*
        Jews
United States
    anti-Semitism in, 30, 54, 68
    civil rights, 64, 72
    Civil War, 63, 64, 72
    Confederacy, 62, 63, 64, 66, 68, 71,
        72, 73, 74

death penalty, 64
Declaration of Independence, 66
disunity of, xviii
and guns, 64
Ku Klux Klan, 20, 60, 64,
    67–68
lynching in, 63, 73, 74
racism in, 60–68 *passim*, 71–74
    passim
    acknowledgement/denial of,
        73–74
    Uncle Tom's Cabin, 72
slavery, 64
and women, xvii
see also alt-right; Black Lives
    Matter; Trump, Donald;
    and under Holocaust;
    repetition
Untermenschen, 1, 21, 47
USSR, 1, 5, 22, 38, 39
    see also Cold War; Communism;
        Eastern Bloc

Varoufakis, Yanis, 49
Vezmar, Marija, x
Vienna Psychoanalytic Society, 28

walls as metaphors, xvii, 39
war
    in Middle East, 31, 41, 47
    psychic legacy of, 25, 6,
        31, 48
    see also asylum; First World War;
        Isis; Nazi Germany; refugees;
        Second World War; *and under*
        United States
Weidel, Alice, xvi
Winnicott, Donald, 59–60, 61
    see also good-enough
women's rights, xvii, 43
    see also misogyny
Woods, Grant, 71, 72
writing, x, 25, 57, 58, 76
    see also language; nursery rhymes;
        stories

xenophobia, xvi, 25, 34, 37, 41–42,
    46–49
passim
        attacks on migrants, 2
        see also nationalism; racism;
            and under group dynamics;
            immigration
Xi Jinping, President, xix

Yang, Yuan, xix
Yazidi, 31–32, 47, 48
Young, James E., 15

Zimbabwe, xvi
Zipes, Jack, 28
Žižek, Slavoj, 41, 42, 47
Zuckerman, Yithak "Antek", 35